PROTECTING INFORMATION ON LOCAL AREA NETWORKS

PROTECTING
INFORMATION ON
LOCAL AREA NETWORKS

James A. Schweitzer

AMERICAN SOCIETY FOR INDUSTRIAL SECURITY
1625 PRINCE STREET
ALEXANDRIA, VA 22314
(703) 519-6200

Butterworths
Boston   London   Durban   Singapore   Sydney   Toronto   Wellington

Library of Congress Cataloging-in-Publication Data

Schweitzer, James A., 1929–
  Protecting information on local area networks /
James A. Schweitzer.
      p.   cm.
  Bibliography: p.
  Includes index.
  1. Local area networks (Computer networks)—Security
measures.
I. Title.
TK5105.7.S39   1988
004.6′ 8—dc19   87–17219
    ISBN 0–409–90138–5

British Library Cataloguing in Publication Data

Schweitzer, James A.
  Protecting information on local area networks.
  1. Local area networks (Computer networks)
  2. Data protection
I. Title
  658.4′ 78   TK5105.7
  ISBN 0–409—90138–5

Butterworth Publishers
80 Montvale Avenue
Stoneham, MA 02180

10 9 8 7 6 5 4 3 2 1

Printed in the United States of America

To Art Axelrod, Carl Grovanz, Myra Johnson,
Paul Kittredge, and all others who have contributed
to the development and implementation
of electronic information security at
Xerox Corporation, 1977–1987.

And to Brian Hollstein and Dick Randazzo,
who have provided us with consistent
management support.

Contents

Introduction

Information has become a valuable resource. Not only is information costly to produce and maintain in a usable form at the right time and place, but it is also crucial to maintaining market share and competitive position in a technological world. Many experts (see, for example, Diebold 1979 and Naisbitt 1982) conclude that information is among the most valuable business resources.

Although networks allow us to make better use of information, the large number of network-connected devices poses a serious threat to information quality. Thousands of people are now connected to business networks, with potential access to information bases. There is a churning of information as these system users change data or move information around. A critical problem is how to manage the valuable information flowing across many networks to hundreds or thousands of employees (and outsiders).

Some idea of this challenge can be gained from considering that one large company has more than fifty individual networks with thousands of connected employees. Similarly, a leading computer manufacturer has networks connecting fifteen hundred mainframe computers with two hundred thousand workstation or terminal users.

We can infer two things from such networks. First, almost everyone who owns a microcomputer with a communications connection is physically connected to everyone else, by virtue of the worldwide telecommunications grid. All those computer users may not be logically connected, but that separation is likely the result of a lack of standards rather than a control effort by management. Second, protecting the information passed through this grid requires careful planning and an immense educational and motivational effort by business managers.

USING NETWORKS IN BUSINESS

Before we consider appropriate management actions to ensure some control over the use of networks and the business information resource, we should look at the various types of networks and why they are being expanded at such a rapid pace.

Today's microcomputers and highly efficient communications systems constitute an economic driver that encourages management to invest in more business networks. The economic driver results from these factors:

1.   Administrative work is essentially a process of communication of information. Analysis of almost any office job will show that it consists of developing, collecting, modifying, and distributing information. All "knowledge workers"—

that is, those persons whose contribution to the business consists of nonphysical products—work at information tasks. These people tend to be the most highly paid and most important employees in a business. A study by Booz Allen & Hamilton concluded that skilled professionals in the United States were paid $400 billion in 1979; clerical workers received only $125 billion. Hence, a 15 percent improvement in productivity from managers and professionals would save a lot more money than would an equivalent improvement for secretaries (Yourdon 1986). New applications of computing and communications will tend to spread throughout those employee groups that have not traditionally had office equipment. These are the decision makers, analysts, and professionals who have been wedded to the pencil and calculator. No more!

2.   Administrative costs are the fastest rising portion of business overhead. The most promising opportunity to reduce administrative costs is through the use of automation systems for knowledge workers. The payoff level, where system costs are justified by a reduction in administrative costs, is being driven lower and lower by the continually improving cost-performance ratio of microcomputing and communications systems (Strassmann 1985).

3.   Highly competitive worldwide marketplaces, especially for high-technology industries, make current information a critical need. Business leaders see automation as a means of delivering strategic decision-base information at the time and place needed. Networks are the key to this service.

4.   Communications costs are declining rapidly in many cases; for instance, the cost of a four-minute call from New York to Los Angeles during business hours fell 26 percent from 1983 to 1986. The fact that telecommunications price reductions are not consistent across all applications is more than offset by computing functionality delivered by local area networks (LANs).

Basic data processing is no longer the answer to management needs for control and information. Rather, traditional information systems are now being integrated with communications technology to create vast networks of computers. In addition, most critical, time-sensitive business information now spends a good portion of its life cycle in electronic form.

THE NETWORKS

This book is not a tutorial on network technology, but every business manager should be aware of the various network options available for both intersite and intrasite communications and the security risks involved in each application.

Intersite Data Communications

Because of the huge investments required to establish a viable communications system, most intersite business network traffic travels over circuits (land lines and radio links) provided by the communications utilities (in the United States, these include AT&T and GTE; in Europe, the PTTs and British Telephone). These public carriers provide various classes of service, including conditioned data lines and packet-switched services. Selection from among the alternatives is usually based on volume of traffic and quality of service required.

Value-added providers resell the communications utilities' capacity after adding special features such as packaging and delivery services. Private carriers also offer network services. One example is a railroad that has used its right-of-way to lay fiber-optic cable connecting the larger cities. Some of the capacity of the optical net is used for railway signals and other traffic, while the excess capacity is sold to businesses.

Sometimes a network, when leased by a business, will be referred to as a private network, although this might not be strictly true. A company usually pays for a logical circuit, not a physical wire, radio relay, or satellite. The seller can then switch traffic among various network alternatives, making sure the capacity remains constant. In some cases, the user does lease specific circuits and can identify the circuit numbers for purposes of traffic analysis. This does not always mean, however, that the physical identity of the circuit is constant.

Computer manufacturers have provided special network architectures (essentially, collections of communications protocols) to improve the efficiency of sets of computers and devices connected via communications lines. IBM's Systems Network Architecture, or SNA, sets specification standards for the devices and services of a data network. Similarly, Digital Equipment Corporation's DECNET establishes interconnection protocols and requirements. A critical problem today is the inability to connect networks and equipment from various suppliers.

In 1981 the International Standards Organization (ISO) adopted the Open Systems Interconnection Reference Model. This model provides for eight layers of architecture to be used in defining the functions required for all communications systems. Eventually, when widely implemented, the ISO model should ease the problem of interconnection of various communications facilities and equipment.

Intrasite Data Communications

While it has long been possible to connect computers and terminal devices located in one building or in a collection of nearby buildings using telephone circuits, really efficient communications within a site were first delivered by the local area networks, or LANs. These networks allow high-speed, high-volume concurrent interconnections among large numbers of workstations (microcomputers), central processors, and communications gateways. The latter allow further communications with outside public networks and, via those facilities, with other LANs and computers.

The number of LANs is growing rapidly. In 1985 and 1986, the number of LAN connections in the United States increased by more than 200 percent. The installed LAN-connected unit base (mostly microcomputers) grew from 735,000 units to 2,383,000 units during that same time. The use of digital private branch exchanges (PBXs), an alternative to LANs in some situations, also increased markedly in that same period. The LAN is generally considered superior, however, in terms of potential for business data handling applications (Ellison and Pritchard 1986).

A brief consideration of two LANs offered by widely known suppliers might help explain what a LAN is and how it works.

Xerox Network System and Ethernet

Xerox Network System (XNS) presents an architecture that distributes microcomputers throughout a network-serviced organization. There is no need for a central processor or host. Fast (10 megabits per second or 1,000,000 bytes per second) data communications are provided among microcomputer workstations (used by people) and servers (systems service machines) connected to the local network using carrier sense multiple access/collision detection methods. The carrier is a baseband cable implementing the Ethernet protocols (also used by Digital Equipment Corporation, or DEC). Communication with external networks, computers, and other devices is provided through one of the connected servers, which acts as a controller. In many applications, all the stations (or servers) on the network are replications of one equipment scheme programmed to provide different services. All appropriate standards are implemented to allow connection with equipment and networks of other design.

AT&T Starlan and ISN

ISN is a high-capacity, packet-switched backbone for integrating dispersed and varying devices. Starlan is a one-megabit-per-second baseband LAN for personal computers, file servers, and peripherals. Multiple Starlan networks can be connected via an ISN node. ISN also can provide communications services to outside networks of varying architectures.

DISTRIBUTED PROCESSING

While not strictly a type of network, distributed data processing (DDP) is a relevant concept that uses both centralized and decentralized information systems. Local intelligent terminals or microcomputers are connected to a central mainframe system via a communications network. Part of the information processing load is carried by the remote computers, thus performing the work closer to the originator and also providing for redundancy in case one unit fails. Data are usually forwarded periodically to a central computer, where the company's data base is maintained. Summary reports, invoices, and so forth are then returned from the central site to the distributed processors. The local computers, of course, are also used for various specialized applications unique to each site. Today, 50 percent of large companies have some kind of DDP. This reflects a trend toward decentralized management, found in more than 80 percent of large businesses (Blank 1986). The spectacular growth in personal computing, driven by cheap hardware and obvious benefits, is the driving force behind the application of DDP.

CONCLUSION

The use of LANs with flexible architectures such as those described for XNS and Starlan means that business managers can design, almost without limits, networks configured to meet all business requirements. They can choose from a wide variety of communications services provided by others for connection over long distances by land lines, radio (including satellite communications), or a combination of these. Services can be tailored to volume or quality requirements, and a variety of such services is offered by public utilities and value-added marketers. Further, business managers can also invest in substantial communications facilities within a building or set of buildings. Most often, these facilities are LANs, special high-speed integrated systems of terminal devices and cables.

Current networks involve the integration of office systems with personal and departmental computing. The rapid development of network-supporting technologies and applications reflects an apparently insatiable demand for connectivity. The host of new technologies and innovative network systems applications, along with the changing work structure and relationships, are altering the ways in which business operates (Kirkley 1986).

The selection and installation of a network is only one part of the management task. In this book, we will consider how management can gain control of the valuable network-serviced information resources now generally available. We will see that the information resource is sometimes wasted or exposed through poorly planned, widespread employee use of computing and communications, and through broadly authorized access to business information bases. Within a short period of time, almost all employees (and perhaps others less welcome) will have access to at least a portion of a business's information base, usually network-connected in electronic form. Our ability to manage and control this valuable yet widely accessed resource is the subject of this book.

PART I

Background

ONE

Understanding Today's Computer Networks

Digital Equipment Corporation founder Ken Olsen, quoted in the *New York Times,* September 4, 1986: "You start with the network, then you hang the computers on later."

"We need to adopt the realities of today's technology: that computing power is cheaper and more expendable than people power; that the network is of ultimate importance in determining overall systems performance." (Manganelli 1986)

Since the delivery of the first commercial computer in the mid-1950s, computing technology has developed at a startling pace. As computers have become more cost-effective (that is, each year a computer of a given size can perform x additional millions of instructions per second), they have also become cheaper and smaller. H.R. Grosch, a well-known authority on computing, says that computer economies relate directly to computer speeds; that is, to achieve a tenfold improvement in price performance, the computer must work one hundred times as fast (Kang et al. 1986). The microcomputer (the ubiquitous personal computer) has proven that general theory to be true, delivering astonishing computing power to the individual at work, at home, and even on airplanes. The technological breakthrough of being able to place an entire processor on a single mass-produced silicon chip (called very large system integration, or VLSI) has made the microcomputer possible (Blank 1986).

Computing applications have evolved to fit almost every requirement, from basic replacement of routine manual clerical work (such as payroll) to sophisticated process control (oil refining). Recently, imaginative applications have given rise to new businesses and have provided existing businesses the opportunity to

---

This chapter introduces our subject. If you are familiar with computing and networks, you may wish to skip to Chapter Two.

expand their activities. Computers have become such an integral part of daily life that our present era is often referred to as the Computer or Information Age.

Today we see a wide variety of powerful computer hardware, from the number-crunching supercomputer to the tiny lap-top portable, with an endless array of applications software, from the word-processing package to the complex programs running an automated steel mill. And the cost per million instructions processed per second (the "MIPS" discussed in computer articles) continues to go down.

Imagine all those computers, large and small, working away at applications. If they each worked individually, the benefits would be far less than optimal. The one factor that makes all these uses of the computer possible, and so attractive, is intercomputer communications.

COMMUNICATIONS BRINGS ADDED VALUE TO COMPUTING

Mainframe computers are being connected to other mainframes and to distant minicomputers, microcomputers, and workstations in a rapidly growing network of high-speed communications lines. In his book *Computer Networks,* Andrew Tanenbaum identifies some good reasons for this (Tanenbaum 1981):

- Business computers that were initially placed to serve the processing requirements of one site are being connected so that executives can quickly call up summaries of data for companywide management purposes.
- Business recognizes that, with the decreasing costs of communications, companies can reap important benefits by making data base information available to anyone, anywhere, when he or she needs it. The individual user, however, should not have to go to the trouble of preparing applications programs or getting expert technical help. The real promise of a business data base is that of sharing current, reliable information. Effective networks, smart workstations, and powerful data base software make this promise a reality (Curtice 1986).
- The reliability of a company's information processing infrastructure can be enhanced by backing up facilities via communications lines.
- The impressive cost performance of microcomputers (also known as personal computers, or PCs) means that data can be processed at the site where it is generated, resulting in more accuracy, and then forwarded to company headquarters on a network, perhaps using otherwise idle time at night.
- A network of intelligent workstations, connected through local and wide area networks, can provide a powerful information exchange medium for all the company's managers. Message (or electronic mail) systems can allow persons thousands of miles apart to coauthor documents, sign off or modify engineering specifications, and exchange messages in a few seconds.
- Microprocessors have a vastly superior price-performance ratio than main-

frames. Although big computers are ten times faster, they may cost a thousand times as much per unit of computing as personal computers.

A *computer network* is an interconnected collection of autonomous computers or a set of computers using common protocols. Some are enormous and complex; the Digital Equipment Corporation operates a network with 60,000 users in 250 locations spread across 29 countries. Certain computer networks might be called *distributed computing systems;* these are networks of computers that share a common operating system. (Xerox Corporation's Internet is an example of such a system, which is comprised of a set of LANs interconnected by a wide area network.) Other networks of computers are called *distributed processing systems;* these share common applications and software but may have different operating systems.

Finally, Tanenbaum (1981) points out that increased reliability can be gained by connecting computers; if one fails, another can pick up the load. Also, the relative price of communications services versus computer hardware is an important consideration. Communications has become inexpensive over the past fifteen years, the same time frame in which the cost of microcomputers has fallen sharply. Thus, the cost of a network is most attractive when measured against the potential business benefits.

TYPES OF COMPUTERS

If we consider current computer use in a simplified way, we see that there are three general types or sizes of computers, although the groups do overlap. Further, we see that most of these computers are now connected by some kind of network.

The general types of computers are mainframes, minicomputers, and microcomputers. Mainframes are large, high-volume, high-speed data processors, which are almost always found in data centers with specialized operating staffs. The work processed on mainframe computers usually consists of data base and high-volume records processing. Mainframe computers are typically connected to wide area networks, for subsequent connection with LANs or other mainframes. In some applications, such as time-sharing uses, the mainframe services various dumb terminals. Mainframes are usually separated from the communications network by a front-end processor, which controls communications and also can provide access security.

Minicomputers are smaller, often specialized high-speed computers used in research, engineering, and other single-purpose environments. Usually most of the minicomputer load is for pure (mathematical) computing. In many applications, minicomputers work in networks with intelligent workstations and terminals.

Microcomputers are very small desktop or portable computers used at work, at home, and while traveling for financial analysis, word processing, and as professional workstations. Most units connected in a LAN are actually microcomputers that act as "servers" with specialized tasks or as general purpose workstations. The personal computer is one type of microcomputer.

A fourth device, the terminal, is not really a computer, although when connected to a computer network, it takes on many of the same attributes, being able to retrieve information and to make use of the processing power of a central mainframe or minicomputer. The terminal, however, cannot do processing, so its uses are limited in potential information activities.

BENEFITS FROM NETWORKING COMPUTERS

While all computers offer important potential benefits to businesses, the real efficiency occurs when they are tied together in networks (Strassmann 1985). Interconnection of computers has the following implications:

1. Microcomputer-using individuals can retrieve data from large data bases on mainframe computers or minicomputers, can make use of the tremendous power of those larger machines, and can process retrieved information locally using programs written and run on the microcomputer.
2. Terminal users can access the central processor directly to retrieve or add data from or to central disk files. They also can use the power of the larger central computer to perform complex calculations that would otherwise be extremely time-consuming.
3. Microcomputer users can exchange data files, messages, and documents with any other microcomputer or terminal owner connected to an appropriate network.
4. Mainframe computers, minicomputers, microcomputers, and terminals can exchange data, messages, and documents.

One example of the advantages of intercomputer communications is an engineering department where various professionals are working on the design of a new product. Without leaving his or her workstation (a network-connected microprocessor), an engineer can perform various calculations, change schedules and drawings, coordinate and obtain approval of those changes with others working on the product, send drawings or messages to colleagues around the world, and print out paper copies of documents. Computer-aided engineering (CAE), manufacturing (CAM), and design (CAD) are illustrations of powerful systems using networked microprocessors and minicomputers.

Similarly, accountants, financial analysts, scientists, manufacturing supervisors, managers, executives, and secretaries can process data, create documents, send messages, file information, retrieve information from central data bases, process data, and do many other business tasks at electronic speeds. On a LAN these applications may involve filing, data retrieval, message, and computing services.

NETWORK TECHNOLOGY AND APPLICATIONS

The terms *local area network, distributed system,* and *server* are relatively new. It is important that the manager responsible for protecting business information understand the kinds of equipment that will be assembled and connected in to-day's business networks. The unique characteristics and astounding capabilities of this new equipment mean that special, imaginative security measures are required.

Computing power and data storage capabilities are moving into the hands of the users, and the traditional network form is changing. Not long ago, computer network applications served only to deliver a slice of a computer's capability to a user at a dumb terminal at a relatively slow speed (appropriately referred to as *time-sharing*). Networks now are being used as high-speed data pipes, connecting mainframe computers and various types of microcomputers (workstations and/or personal computers). The networks are usually carrying packets that de-liver documents, entire files, and messages. This change in capability, traffic, and service demands means that networks must be able to handle huge volumes of data at high speeds and must be able to cope with peak volumes at certain times. Interconnectivity and replication of network links are required to ensure the needed flexibility.

Many networks now have built-in intelligence; for example, protocol conver-sion is often offered as a network service. Many devices that in the past required a tedious conversion from one signal format or protocol to another can now be simply plugged in. Users may soon be able to switch back and forth among workstations—say from an IBM PC to a Wang word processor—or to access different makers' mainframes from a single desktop workstation.

Eventually, all data processors and networks will have protocol compatibil-ity. The basic plan will probably be the ISO's Open Systems Interconnection Ref-erence Model. The standard defines various levels of network processes; once the various network protocols are standardized, increased internetwork connectivity and operability will result. Networks will soon be conglomerations of mainframe computers, personal workstations, special purpose minicomputers, and servers (Herman 1986).

Quarterman and Hoskins (1986) suggest that there are five basic kinds of networks, based on purpose, administration, and funding. These are:

1. Research networks supported by government grants and used by various groups in universities or the military. Examples include ARPANET, CSNET, and MILNET.
2. Company networks developed by businesses and often consisting of intercon-nected LANs, or internets, which may also connect with central processors. Some of these have tens of thousands of users, twenty or thirty mainframe computers, and tens of thousands of miles of circuits in intercontinental grids.

3. Cooperative networks that serve groups of users with common interests. These include BITNET, NETNORTH, and EARN.
4. Commercial networks that provide value-added services to their customers, who are charged a user fee. TYMNET and TELENET are examples. These are public service networks, some operated by common carriers.
5. Metanetworks, planned for the future to connect several existing networks. CSNET is currently being implemented (Quarterman and Hoskins 1986).

Some major business internets (connections of various local area and wide area networks) are shown in the following table.

Network Name	Continents Covered	Hosts Attached	Users/Workstations Attached
DEC Easynet	4	10,000	60,000
IBM	4	20,000	100,000
Xerox Internet	3	1,000	12,000

Source: Quarterman and Hoskins 1986, p. 936, and other estimates by author.

CONSIDERING A LOCAL AREA NETWORK

Some readers may not be familiar with the new networks. Others may not be familiar with the model used in this book, which is the Xerox Network System (XNS) using the Ethernet protocol. Let's briefly review what makes up a LAN, how it operates, and the information vulnerabilities inherent in such an operation.

Local area networks are now the most common way of implementing a distributed processing system, one that delivers a range of computing power to various workstations and devices connected together. The U.S. Bureau of Standards provides the following definition of a LAN:

> In general, these networks are deployed in small geographic areas such as an office complex, building, or campus. Typically, they are owned, operated and managed locally rather than by a common carrier. Bus, ring, star and mesh topologies that support the interconnection of up to hundreds of devices communicating by packet transmissions at rates in the 1 to 20 megabit range are not unusual.

Major business networks, made of interconnected local and wide area networks (called *internets*), are operated by Digital Equipment Corporation (Easynet), IBM (VNET), AT&T (USENET), and Xerox (Internet). Many other businesses have similar networks. Communication among the networks is possible through shared connection points, the most obvious being via the government-sponsored ARPANET (Quarterman and Hoskins 1986).

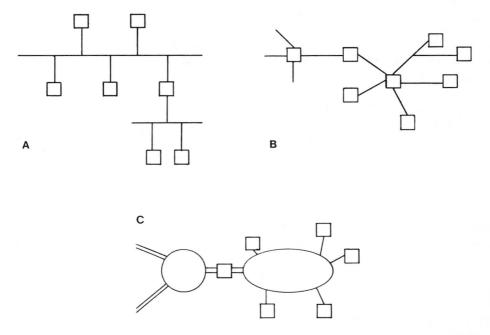

Figure 1.1   Local area network topologies. *A* Bus network. *B* Star network. *C* Ring network.

Most LANs have a ring, star, or bus topology, as shown in Figure 1.1. The cable or wire that connects units to the network are typically twisted pair circuits (telephone wires), coaxial cable (shielded cable), or fiber optics. Fiber optics is just coming into use and offers better security against eavesdropping than the other two types. The way the messages are carried across the cable is called baseband or broadband. Simply put, baseband carries one data stream; broadband can carry several, at different frequencies.

The topology of a network may directly affect the kinds of security vulnerabilities we must protect against (Cotnoir 1986). Consider the data flow on a star network versus that on a bus topology. In the latter case, every message must pass every node; not so on the star. Also, the baseband or broadband cable implementation may change the security risk; the costs to tap each are different, and the efforts to unscramble the data flowing also are different. Generally, baseband allows easier access, but broadband potentially delivers more information; in either case, the work involved in a tap is not simple.

A LAN is often connected with other LANs and other computer networks inside the company, and with distant networks of various kinds using public utility long lines or truck networks. Many LANs are now interconnected in sophisticated, distributed systems that offer universal connectivity and distribution of services.

Parts of a Local Area Network

A LAN is made up of the network cables, workstations (used by humans), and various kinds of servers (used by the LAN system). In more detail, these LAN parts are:

- Workstations, which are the human interface units. These may be personal computers, word processors, or high-powered professional workstations with graphics capabilities. Conceptually, a LAN workstation is a replication of all other workstations and shares the same operating system. In practical application, many of the units or entities of a LAN are different and are connected to the LAN using special adapters.
- Servers, which are the microcomputers that provide the LAN services, such as clearinghouse and security controls, printing services, internetwork communications services, and filing services.
- The network or wire, which connects the network entities into a physical whole. The LAN is also an integral system logically because it shares an operating system. In the Xerox LAN (and in others, such as DEC's) the wire is the Ethernet system.

Although the technical details of one kind of network are different from the details of others (for instance, IBM's SNA, DEC's Digital Network Architecture, and Hewlitt Packard's Distributed Systems Network are all different), the external operating processes and hence the security considerations are similar.

Functions of a Local Area Network

Conceptually, the XNS is a distributed computing system. That is, in its pure form it consists of a number of like computers connected together that share an identical operating system. Other networks may be distributed processing systems, in which different computers or devices using different operating or communications systems are interconnected, often by use of special protocol conversion interface machines.

Most people think of office systems when they consider LANs, but LANs can be used for scientific, engineering, and manufacturing applications as well. In a typical application, closely located facilities are connected to form "campus" LANs. Campuses are connected via leased telecommunications circuits or public utility data networks. Within the business facilities, employees connect to the LAN by using various workstations. There are many types of workstation, but the most common is the personal computer (for example, the Xerox 6065 personal computer or the IBM PC-AT). The Xerox 6085 or 8010 professional workstations and workstations from other manufacturers also are available. In modern LANs, workstations from any number of manufacturers may be connected. The LAN may also be directly connected to mainframe computers; for

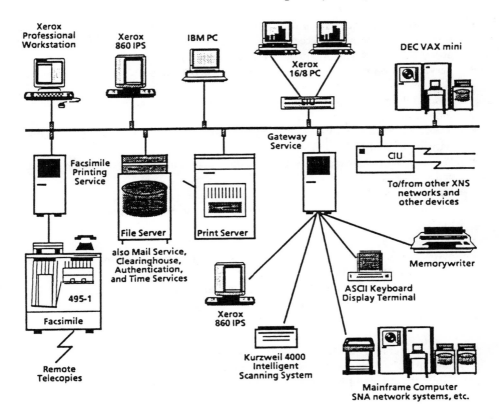

Figure 1.2   A typical local area network. (Courtesy of the Xerox Corporation.)

instance, in the XNS, connections to DEC VAX computers are common. The XNS LAN also provides connection with various network architectures, including IBM and DEC networks. Users may connect with the LAN through dial-up services from any telephone.

Using the facilities of the XNS distributed system, LAN users can electronically create, edit, merge, file, and print documents, as well as review and change documents or sets of documents. Programmers can write applications software, and individual data bases can be built and maintained from data retrieved from central data base computers for local processing. These data may then be sent back to the mainframe files. Users are connected with one another through a global electronic message system, which can transfer documents or files to any location in the world. Figure 1.2 shows a typical LAN.

The distributed computing network called XNS includes various workstations and servers. The workstations provide the human interface with the network; the servers provide the network services. The workstations may include the following:

- Professional workstations that allow creation of documents with graphics, provide multiwindow screen displays, offer powerful communication, and allow the use of various programmable functions.
- Personal computers that provide for local processing and disk storage plus a rich array of network services.
- Nonintelligent 3270 terminal devices, connected through special low-speed interface units.
- So-called "smart" copiers, which allow document transmission and creation with high-quality laser printing.
- Word processors that can send and file documents via the network servers, at local or remote sites.
- Various special units, such as high-speed plotters or bulk document printers, which can be driven from network-connected units to produce finished print pieces.

The workstations have high-capacity storage built-in, in the form of fixed disks; they also may provide floppy disk storage.

Other network units, called servers, are probably the same computers found in the professional workstations, but they are programmed to provide special services. Among the servers are the following:

- Print servers, which drive printers attached to the network. Usually these high-quality printers can handle graphics as well as a variety of typefaces. The network printers are typically shared among users in a work group or location.

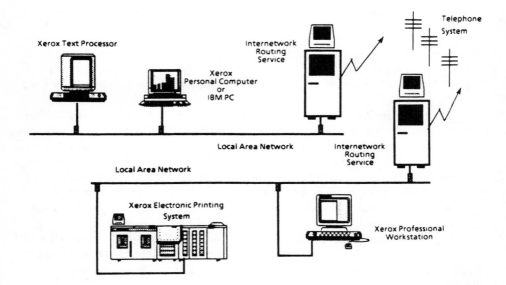

Figure 1.3   Xerox LAN with connections to other nets.

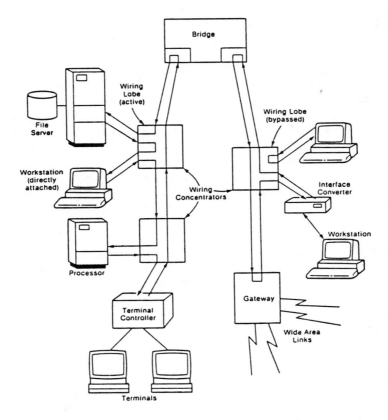

Figure 1.4   IBM LAN with connections to other nets.

- File servers, which provide users with high-capacity remote storage on fixed disks. Files can be accessed locally or from any distant point on the network.
- Clearinghouse and communications servers, which provide local network security, clearinghouse (user authentication) controls, and "mail" address location and distribution services. These servers also provide internetwork connection services, which handle the speed and protocol conversions necessary for connection with public utility telecommunications.

Figure 1.3 shows a typical XNS local area network with an interface to a public utility for connection with other LANs or with other network types. Figure 1.4 shows an application of the IBM Token Ring network, which uses a different protocol but involves much the same security considerations.

What a Local Area Network Does

Consider the LAN as an electronic office. The workstation is the desk, and the disk files at the workstation are the in-desk files of documents. The file server's central files are the files maintained by the secretary at a central station in the office. The communications server is the mail room; the print server is the copy room and typewriter.

The employee using a LAN may have a workstation display that visually represents physical items in the office. These representations are called icons. The icons might represent file cabinets, file folders, documents, or messages. Icons also represent various services provided by the LAN, such as printers, out boxes, and in boxes (for sending and receiving messages). By pointing to an icon with the cursor, the user may move it, combine it with other items, print it, or dispatch it via a communications service.

Certain icons represent powerful macro programs, which perform specified functions, such as dialing into another network. Spreadsheet software may be available as an icon. Documents might be retrieved from a number of distant file servers, assembled into a file folder icon, and then transmitted to some distant point, perhaps on another continent, in a few minutes' time. The LAN really provides an electronically integrated office across a campus, a city, or a nation. The communications capabilities inherent in the LAN are mind-boggling. Clearly, when people have access to a LAN, they also have a tremendous amount of power. When planning security, we must consider that this power could be misused.

NETWORK VULNERABILITIES

Business networks are all physically connected; that is, all significant networks (at least all those we know about) use the public utility networks (such as AT&T and GTE in the United States, British Telecom and the PTTs in Europe), and/or specialized value-added networks such as TELENET or TYMNET for long-distance trunk connections and local network interconnections.

Of course, most of these networks are logically separate; that is, by design or chance, they use different protocols or contain controls that supposedly prevent traffic from passing from one to the other. Practical experience shows, however, that clever people can almost always find a way to communicate through the labyrinth of connections that makes up today's telecommunications grid. For example, message traffic is common between various parties at DEC, Xerox, NCR, and other companies. No formal connection exists; but people have figured out ways to make one (Quarterman and Hoskins 1986). Many other companies' LANs may be informally connected with your company's network, allowing unauthorized persons access to your files.

An even more dangerous situation exists with regard to dial-up services to a LAN. A dial-up connection requires only that the person attempting such a connection has a suitable terminal device, a modem (to convert digital signals to the analog form used by the telephone system), and a telephone.

Once connected to any network (wide or local area), the caller has the potential to access files on many other networks. Further, the original network accessed has very little reliable means to ascertain the identity, and hence the rights, of the caller once an entry is achieved. As we have seen, an employee accessing a network from a connected workstation must authenticate his or her identity via the network clearinghouse before connection takes place. The telephone caller may, however, have no workstation identity or location; the proof of identity and privileges in this case must be at the file level and can leave much to be desired in a security sense.

Telecommunications traffic passing over interconnected LANs and other networks has varying vulnerability to information loss or exposure. For example:

- Traffic on a LAN travels at an extremely high speed, and a simple tap (that is, a connection without standard network equipment) of the wire carrying the signal would be technically difficult. However, a technically correct connection using a transceiver unit, cable, and workstation is not difficult to achieve in a physical sense.
- Traffic leaving a communications server and passing onto the utility network may have only minimal speed, such as 9600 baud, and could be copied with a simple wiretap and tape recorder. Telephone junction boxes and equipment rooms may not be physically secure to the same degree as server rooms.
- After passing through a utility (telephone) switch (usually at the central telephone exchange), the signal may be multiplexed at very high speeds (such as 56000 baud), and a tap would be prohibitively expensive.
- Once on the wide area network, information is vulnerable to wiretapping, usually where wires are connected to junction boxes or frames. Many times these attacks take place on the premises of the company. Passive interception may occur when traffic travels over radio links; these are now so common that almost any message has a good chance of being transmitted via radio on some part of its journey.

This variation in threats at different points in the network system means that business managers must be extremely careful about using interconnected networks for sensitive information. While the LAN may be physically secure—for example, located entirely within one building—a message sent to another company location may be exposed when it passes over an ordinary telephone line on a public street. Sometimes it is impossible to determine exact routings for internetwork traffic. Our conclusion from all this is that we must have encryption services (Chapter Four) for sensitive information to be communicated outside areas under our direct physical control. Sometimes encryption may be required within a LAN, such as when one part of a building containing network circuit cables is leased to outside tenants.

Networks and Software Increase Risks

The arrival of the personal computer generated a need for network software to provide a transparent means for PCs to direct disk access requests to the disk server. Portable software such as CP/M and MS/DOS makes this job easier, since it is designed for disk subsystems. Various systems developers are working on microcomputer software that will allow movement toward "open" corporate networks of PCs. Host computers will be tied to a standard net (such as Ethernet) connected with workstations and PCs via either the XNS or ISO protocol. A PC may then call any other component of the interconnected LANs and act as a peer in the network (Davidson and Huntington 1985).

Securing a Local Area Network

Generally, as the number of devices connected, the number of users, and the range of actions allowed users increase, the security vulnerabilities of a network increase geometrically. In other words,

number of devices × number of users × user privileges = risk.

This is oversimplified no doubt, but the message is there.

The points of attack possible in a secured data center with one computer can probably be counted on one's fingers. But in a network of hundreds of workstations, potential points of attack add up to big numbers. Consider the following:

- Every dumb terminal connected.
- Every terminal connected to an interface device.
- Every computer connected.
- Every circuit in the network.
- Every services device in the network.
- Every dial-up access device.

All of these are potential points for attempting a penetration or for unauthorized activity.

Most of the attacks that we read about are active, meaning that they involve someone who uses a program, a terminal, or a microcomputer to try to gain access for unauthorized purposes. But some types of attack require no direct connection with the network at all, such as the interception of satellite radio signals or of emanated signals from visual displays. Active attacks may well involve an authorized person at an authorized network unit or node.

NETWORK RISKS AND SECURITY MEASURES

Serious security vulnerabilities result from the connection of many workstations, personal computers, and mainframe data base computers, using networks where traffic may follow various routes. Consider a workstation or personal computer. We can project these network risk levels:

Configuration	Risk Level
Stand-alone microcomputer	Minimum (provided user takes prudent care; see Chapter 7)
Directly wired microcomputer	Moderate (less risk of dial-up attack)
Networked microcomputer	High (because of difficulty in authenticating all users)

In a network situation our goal must be to provide secure host computers, secure links to any of the workstations or devices connected, and secure workstations and devices. At the same time, we cannot compromise the business efficiency that the technology of communications and computing has provided; management simply will not allow it. (Details of implementing security are given in Chapters Three and Four.)

Basic network security must be established at the file level, with activity authorizations determined and enforced for each authenticated user. But we would prefer to stop an unauthorized person as far away from the valuable information as possible. Local area network authentication systems often allow for proof of identity in the sign-on process. At another level, the network may control a user's access by means of a network control center, usually part of a wide area network management system.

The workstations and servers also require physical security protection. Workstations require a level of physical protection suitable to the sensitivity of the information processed or displayed thereon. Servers usually require some special physical security controls equivalent to those in a data center. Communications or clearinghouse servers should be in a controlled area; they are the control center for the local network. Access should be allowed only to specially authorized people who have a need to work with those devices.

Print servers and their connected printers also should be in a controlled area to maintain the security of the output documents, or some physical control should be provided, such as locked bins. If the documents produced do not require a significant level of protection, network users should be instructed on prompt pickup of output documents when those papers contain sensitive information. The network-connected printer is probably a severe security exposure in most cases when it is placed in a room or hallway where passers-by can access the output.

Logical security controls (that is, those access control measures implemented through software and hardware functions) are essential for a LAN, for both workstations and servers. Workstations typically have a desktop, the personal work space provided for the individual user to store current documents (information) and to do work. This desktop area should be protected by a user password. The password is held and authenticated by the clearinghouse server. Passwords usually are stored and moved about in encrypted form. The desktop and the local workstation fixed disk are the most secure places for information storage on a LAN, because they are not usually accessible from other network units.

Servers also are protected by passwords. The access rights to these critical devices are usually given to system administrators, who service the LAN by performing various technical adjustments and providing backup files.

Technical Aspects of Logical Security in the Xerox XNS

An open, distributed system poses severe security problems, since access to the system resources may be relatively easy to achieve for technically astute persons who may or may not be authorized users and for others who may dial in from distant or unknown places. The XNS provides two kinds of control. Access control mechanisms are built into both workstations and servers, and an authentication process helps users and servers identify each other reliably. The authentication protocol provides a secure authentication service that assigns both users and services encrypted passwords; further, the clocks in the various system elements are synchronized. Strong and weak authentication levels are provided; this allows XNS users to select the level, and hence the cost, of security appropriate to a particular information value. Figure 1.5 illustrates the strong authentication process.

Procedural security for workstations and servers consists of the assignment of network rights and the monitoring of the proper use of those rights. This is a most essential task. To understand the procedural security requirements of a LAN, consider the kinds of privileges allowed:

Highest level: The network operating system administrator. This person can promulgate operating system changes and network software modifications to accommodate network topology changes essential to network operation. A company would typically have only one or two people with this level of privilege.

Second level: The system administrator is a local person responsible for maintaining network services, correcting minor network system or component faults, and providing file backup for contingency purposes. Since the system administrator can register new network members (users) and can set user passwords, this is a very sensitive position. The local system administrator could change the password of an authorized user and thus, at least temporarily, gain access to that user's central files. The administrator could not, however, access the user's desktop files without gaining access to the user's workstation. System administrators require careful selection, training, and supervision.

Lowest level: Passwords permit users to access their own files and any others for which they have been given access rights. Of course, some files may be public, or available to anyone who can access the network.

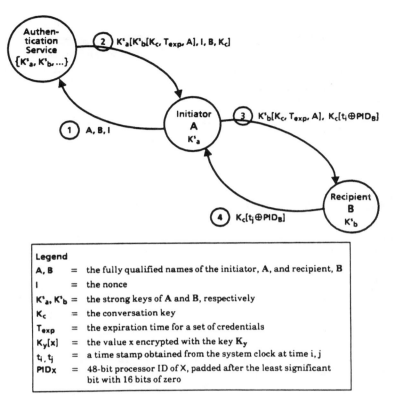

Figure 1.5   XNS strong authentication model. (Courtesy of the Xerox Corporation.)

The clearinghouse server controls the accesses to and processes in the network. File servers provide varying user access privileges for the files stored there. Each file drawer (that is, disk space) has an owner registered in the LAN clearinghouse. The owner (or system administrator) can set rights for each user allowed access to the information in that drawer; such rights might include read, move, modify, and so forth. In most cases, a person connected to the network must pass several tests before being allowed access to files. These include the following:

- Is the person requesting access a member of the network on which the requested file resides? (That is, is the network identifier the same for the requester and for the file? In Ethernet, the standard naming is "User name:Domain [local network] name:Network name".)
- Is the requester a member of the same domain as the requested file?
- Is the requester identified on the file's access authorization list?

In XNS, the use of an asterisk in the domain or network spaces in the standard network address (for example, "Records:*:*") is the default for that portion of the address; the use of the asterisk in the domain and file name sections of the network address makes that file available to anyone on the company network. It is often seen as a convenience to use public file addresses, but it is obviously a severe security vulnerability.

LANs may allow the use of "guest" accounts when the business situation indicates a need for persons to access the network resources without formal registration as a user. An example of such a case is during customer demonstrations. Like the asterisk address default, the use of guest accounts is a severe security risk and must be well controlled. These problems are addressed in detail in Chapters Three and Four.

Access rights also can be specified according to what actions an accessor may take. Such rights include delete, move, read, alter, add, and so on.

Securing a Wide Area Network

Packaged network management and control systems now offer security features similar to the access management systems described in the network security standards (see Chapter Six), and providing automated activity logging. Systems such as Avante-Guarde's Net Guard control access to network nodes, which might be workstations. Usually, the controlled nodes are access points to subnetworks or clusters of devices. The network control center can monitor activities across network control points and can establish access rules for entry from outside the company's network.

Some controls are referred to as port control or callback devices. These are usually subsystems made up of hardware and software that allow the security manager to establish preconditions for connection. For example, the person attempting a connection from a telephone may be required to give an identifier; the port control system then validates this identifier and instructs the caller to disconnect. The security system then calls the identified user at a preset telephone. Access limitations also can be set to restrict access for particular users to specified times of day or to certain ports reserved for a specific application.

The use of port controls or wide area network security systems provides a second or outer level of protection, but file level access control usually also is required. In many cases, the network operator assumes all internode links to be vulnerable to public access; hence, encryption of traffic and file access controls are essential.

THE PERSONAL COMPUTER AND NETWORKS

Chapter Seven discusses security for network-connected personal computers, but the PC deserves mention here. The PC is a very important technological advance, making computing available to the average employee. But it is also a dangerous device when used in an unplanned and unmanaged way. Connection to networks makes security exposure even more severe. And since PCs may be obtained outside the normal computing resources management channels, managers may be unaware of their existence.

The personal computer is a sort of micro data center. From a security viewpoint, it has all the risks and vulnerabilities of a data center, except that the amount of data is much less. When connected to a network, the PC has the stuff that security managers' nightmares are made of. Consider the following:

- Network-connected PC users can download data files from a central processor and then process those files through untested software, producing what many people may accept as official reports.
- Personal computer users can buy, copy, or steal software from any source, including "free" software distributed on so-called electronic bulletin boards, and then use that software to process important business decision data. There is no way to know whether such programs have hidden logical faults, such as trap doors or Trojan horses.
- Personal computer users might access files that should not be available, using the power of the PC to do automatic dial-ups, statistical testing for passwords, programs to spoof security systems, and other penetrations.
- Personal computer users may be able to bypass security systems protecting files belonging to others on a fixed disk by modifying the computer's operating system. After all, the PC user *is* the data center manager for that computer.

William H. Murray, writing in the *IBM Systems Journal,* suggests a set of guidelines for employee behavior in the use of personal computers. Some of those are:

- Users have an obligation to adhere to the spirit as well as the letter of all applicable policies, standards, and laws.
- Use of PCs should be restricted to business purposes.
- Connection with other systems should be only upon approval of the managers of both locations or units.
- Users must be responsible for the security of hardware and data.
- Users must be responsible for information integrity.
- Reports prepared on PCs must indicate the source.
- Users must report all variances from expected equipment or software behavior or from data use or content (Murray 1984).

The personal computer is really a special form of microcomputer workstation, but its cheapness and ready attachment to networks, perhaps by dial-up from home, make it a special security vulnerability.

SOME SECURITY CASES INVOLVING NETWORKS

To finish our discussion of the various networks and their operation, let's consider some actual security cases, which demonstrate the risks involved.

1. A Zyre Company data center in a distant country started up the central computer on a Monday morning. To its surprise, a confidential listing of com-

pany executives' payroll printed out. Investigation showed that the central data center had canceled a print job on the previous Friday. A system regeneration had brought into play an unknown algorithm buried in the operating system, which allocated unfinished jobs to the next available lowest numbered printer. Printer number 1 of the Zyre Company happened to be in a foreign country.

2. An engineer was able to browse through various public files on interconnected networks of the Able Engineering Company. The engineer put together a history of the development of a sensitive new product, including details such as technology selection decisions and market targets. Had the history been exposed, severe damage could have been done to the company, and its rights to various processes could have been compromised.

3. A software expert developed a program to correct errors in network software. The program would propagate itself through the various network machines. When tested, the software did as expected, but then could not be stopped from continuing with unwanted changes without shutting down the entire network.

4. A confidential personnel memorandum was sent to a distribution list (an automatic service of most networks). The wrong list code was used, however, and the memo went to many people who had no need to know that particular information.

5. Computer hackers accessed a business network and eventually were able to modify access control statements in the central computer. The computer had to be shut down to clean out the hackers' programs and to reestablish control.

6. A network administrator's code was carelessly handled. As a result, a person not authorized to have the code purposely damaged and destroyed information files on the network servers. This was done by changing the access code of the authorized user, then changing it back to the original code after the damage was done.

TWO

A Management
Responsibility: Protecting
Information on Networks

A management view of the network information security issue is essential if an effective protection system is to be installed in an operating business. Business requirements always drive security, never the other way around. Furthermore, a top level management approach can be very helpful to the security manager or systems manager concerned with network security for several reasons, including:

- The development of a company information network security policy requires a competent grasp of the management reasons for such.
- Justification of resources for securing a network to senior management demands careful groundwork in language the executives understand. The *information quality* concept developed here has been found useful in this regard.

Some business managers may not yet recognize security as an important, integral element of the business operations process. But those same managers will know that quality information is absolutely essential to the effective management of a competitive business. Quality can be ensured only if information is suitably protected. And information security will be effective only when implemented as part of an overall information resource program. In this chapter we will discuss the management rationale for network information security. This rationale is useful for establishing, with senior management, the need for appropriate security resources, as defined in Chapters Four and Five.

Many managers know that information requires protection. But few have thought through the management decision process that leads to a justification for spending on information security. Later I will specify the security requirements for operating a complex business network. But a prerequisite to implementing such protection measures is support from top management on the business security resource requirements. In this chapter I will start from the beginning to explain a carefully derived management process leading to a decision in favor of providing security for business information on networks.

A CRITICAL BUSINESS REQUIREMENT: INFORMATION QUALITY

In today's business environment, where a competitive edge may depend on correct and timely information, it is essential that the quality of information processed and delivered by computer and network information systems be ensured. Information quality must be a primary concern of every manager responsible for developing applications, providing information processing services, or managing networks, and of every employee using a network-connected workstation.

Business quality information has certain characteristics. These are *integrity, reliability,* and *privacy.*

Integrity   means that the information has accuracy to the degree anticipated by the user, completeness, and freedom from unauthorized change. Note that we do not claim that information can ever be 100 percent free of errors, but quality information is at least as good, or pure, as the user expects. Integrity implies that information has been shielded from gross carelessness and intentional unauthorized change, that it has not been processed through unreliable programs, and that the data have been controlled through various steps in the processing. Such controls may include batch counts, validations, reasonability checks, supervisory inspection, and security protection measures.

Reliability   means that the information is obtainable by the authorized users when and where needed, and that it is delivered free from unauthorized change, destruction, or theft. In the network situation, this implies network system management in a total sense; should a certain network routing be unavailable, the network control system must be able to replace or bypass the missing node or link. Of course, the network infrastructure, the lines, the mainframe computers, and the connected workstations must be protected from a physical or logical attack that could affect data quality or deny the company their use. Also, reliability means that network user files and central data base files are periodically backed up to ensure against a catastrophic loss of data. Major processes must be recoverable, in case of a processing or communications failure, through the use of planned system recovery procedures.

Privacy   is an assurance that the data, in all its forms (written, electronic, mental), is protected from theft and unauthorized observation. In a network this means protection against penetration into controlled network facilities, files, and circuits. When LANs are in use, this vulnerability is severe, as each of the workstations, servers, and circuits must be considered a potential target for unauthorized data observations. Privacy also means that encryption is used to protect sensitive data when in transmission over lines passing through spaces not directly controlled by the information's owner. For high-value data passing through interconnected network circuits, encryption is a priority business requirement.

Information quality is ensured through a carefully defined set of management actions. These embrace the information cycle of data gathering, processing, and use, from original collection through eventual obsolescence. Security is only one of several management actions that are requisite to information quality. Security measures follow logically from a management decision on information quality. These management actions together make up the elements of information quality:

- Management of business information as a critical resource.
- Good systems design to provide efficient information processes.
- Effective management and control of information processing and communication.
- Protection of information in processing and in communication systems.

These elements are discussed in detail below.

MANAGEMENT ACTION 1:
MANAGEMENT OF THE INFORMATION RESOURCE

Management of the business information resource means that the company recognizes information as a critical business resource and takes appropriate actions to manage it. Such actions include:

1. The identification of the business's information base, in terms of those data elements essential to business operations.
2. The valuation or classification of business data elements so as to allow the provision of appropriate protection measures.

The assignment of responsibility for information management follows logically from management's recognizing information as an important and expensive business asset. A suitable organizational structure and definition of information management responsibilities through properly constituted and published directives are essential.

One cannot reasonably get into the process of information valuation and control unless directed to do so; too many important decisions are required, and too many resources are needed, to plunge into the matter casually. The priority, then, is to make senior company officers aware of the issues surrounding computing and communications access.

Other important resources have long been established as important management responsibilities. We have the vice president of personnel, the vice president of materials, and the vice president of treasury. In contrast, information, which is generally agreed to be the most critical business resource today, is usually handled as an orphan. A few progressive companies have high-level information managers (perhaps the director of information management), but often this position is merely a renaming of a job primarily concerned with managing computer applications development and hardware. This is like having a jewelry store where the manager is concerned about the store fixtures and the vault but is unaware of the value of the jewels themselves. Recognizing the importance of information and assigning a top level executive to oversee its use are prerequisites to information management.

Many will ask, "What has this to do with securing information on networks?" The answer is that we must be concerned about protecting information, not the network itself. And we cannot possibly do an effective job of protecting all information. We must have some indication of which business data are really valuable so that limited protection resources can be put in the right places. We also want to make sure that information in hard copy form, usually the output of networks, continues to receive protection. Information management provides the basis for doing these things well.

We recently saw a security policy written for a progressive electronic tool company. The policy said that the company data center would protect all information entrusted to it for processing. In and of itself, such a policy is irrelevant to the business; it may be important to the data center, but the company should be concerned that protection extends to information in all forms, not just in electronic form. Information management sets a structure for protecting the business by ensuring an appropriate level of information quality.

What Constitutes the Essential Information Base?

Before a materials manager begins work, he or she wants to know what materials are in stock and how valuable each item is. Similarly, information management presupposes that we know the stock of information needed to operate our business. We cannot actually count up information items, but we can identify the essential information elements that are critical to our business operation. An information element is a basic piece of information. It may occur in many different places and in mental, written, or electronic form.

A basic information element has these characteristics:

- It is essential to the business.
- It is generated by a primary business function.
- It may occur in various combinations with other data.

Examples of information elements are:

- Employee name (from personnel function, appears in commissions record).
- Customer name (marketing function, appears in credit record).
- Product specifications (engineering function, appears in manufacturing record).
- Accounts receivable (accounting function, appears in general ledger record).

A listing of all the basic information elements essential to a business identifies those information elements that are candidates for management and control. The decision as to whether the company wishes to manage a particular information element depends on its valuation. Of course, new information elements may be developed or recognized, and existing information elements may be used in reports or memos in the course of business operations. In such cases, it is the responsibility of the originating manager to take action to have a value assigned so that, if necessary, the information will receive the proper management and control.

There is an opportunity to achieve important information systems benefits from organizing the business information base. As more and more people see that they can use information delivered via personal computing and networking, information demands will increase. But these requirements for access to central data bases, and the applications in which they will be used, are almost impossible to forecast. It is very important, therefore, that we separate information elements from business applications and that we provide those elements in a form that can be readily accessed for a variety of applications and purposes.

The cost of maintaining redundant information elements in several applications has long been recognized as a problem. Also, data administrators are becoming more concerned with consistency and integrity of data as information is retrieved from central data bases and entered into decision support systems, information centers, and management information systems ("Making Better Use of Your Data" 1986). The real concern is that the data have quality, as we defined it here, whenever and wherever they are used, and that they be relevant to the business objectives. Effective information management works toward these ends by controlling the information resource. Furthermore, good information management also can make systems design more effective. For most businesses, information management is critical for the information age.

Which Information Elements Require Protection?

It is intuitively obvious that certain information, such as payroll data, supplier bids, and customer lists, have a value or may require certain privacy. We know from experience and from prudent reflection that there are some data that reasonable people do not wish to have disclosed. We also can make intuitive judgments about information that has a competitive value. To do the information management job properly, however, decisions on information value must be based on a more formal model.

This value model is based on two criteria:

1. What is the damage to the business if the information is exposed to persons unauthorized to have it?
2. What is the damage to the business if the information is unavailable?

Before we match our list of basic information elements against the value model, we should have a value or classification scheme. That is, we do not want to make a value decision and as a result call a given piece of information "most valuable" or "least valuable." It is more convenient to have classification names, supported by precise definitions, which will indicate to all employees the relative value of a certain information element and, consequently, how much effort should be put forth in controlling that element. The classification of information establishes the basis for all information security activity.

The value model can be further developed to make it more useful. It is helpful to consider that information has subjective and objective value.

Subjective Value

What damage is done to the business if the information is exposed, damaged, or becomes unavailable because of value inherent in the data themselves? This is a subjective criterion. For example, exposure or destruction of customer lists or manufacturing specifications could cause the company to be embarrassed or to lose market share or strategic advantage. This damage results from qualities inherent in the information itself.

Objective Value

What damage is done to the business if the information is not available when required for a critical purpose? This is an objective criterion, depending on qualities or specifications outside the data. For example, if accounting records that by law must be maintained for a number of years are lost, the company could be the object of legal action.

Of course, some information elements will fall into both categories in our value model. Certain personnel records—for example, those having to do with workmen's compensation—might fall into a dual category.

Information Classification Policy

Information management policy should set forth the information classification names and criteria so that value decisions (made from the list of essential information elements) will be consistent and fairly rigorous. Such a policy specification might be set up as follows. (Note: Classification titles used here are given as examples; others used by leading businesses include Business Restricted, Registered, Private, and Personal. It is probably a good idea not to use any governmental security classification titles such as Confidential, Secret, Top Secret, and so on.)

The definitions of the classifications here are very brief and are for illustrative purposes only. Information managers would, no doubt, develop much more com-

Subjective Classifications	Labels		
	Restricted	*Sensitive*	*Private*
Definition	Exposure would seriously damage long-term profit	Exposure would impair profit	Exposure would embarrass employees or job applicants
Objective Classifications	*Deposited*	*Retained*	
Definition	Unavailability would have serious legal or ethical consequences	Unavailability would affect ongoing business operations	

plete and inclusive descriptions to allow effective information classifying actions. The sample information security policy given later in this chapter illustrates the function of classification schemes.

Once developed, the list of classified information elements provides the basis for information security decisions. Some elements (those with High Value classifications) will require intense management effort. Others from the list of basic information elements may require moderate security effort; still others may not be classified at all and thus require no management attention other than the occasional admonition to employees that "all company information is private to the company."

Organization and Responsibilities for Information Management

Conceptually, information management is a major companywide program controlled from the top management levels. In real life, however, programs usually begin as more restricted efforts. Pieces of the information management program can be picked up and adapted to the business situation at hand. Keep in mind one cardinal rule: An information element must be protected in all its forms, at all times, and in all places. Otherwise, the effort is futile.

Generally, organization should be established at three levels. Reporting relationships are unimportant at this stage of the discussion; the functions are the important things.

Top level: Information manager defines the basic information element structure for the business; defines information classification scheme; identifies the "data owner" for each element who will make classification and access authorization decisions; exercises executive control over the business's information resource.

Middle level: Data administration manager establishes the administrative control structure for managing the essential information base; through a data base manager, fixes the optimal arrangement of data in the central data bases (this may involve publication of a data dictionary, which describes the technical makeup of data elements and the standard processes for retrieving them).

Security manager establishes information protection requirements as suitable to the various information classifications assigned; advises information systems technicians on security methods and elements for the total company information system, including networks; participates in the planning process for networks and systems. (A significant level of technical expertise is required here, beyond that usually found in today's security departments.)

Lower level: Information security specialist implements the protection measures required through software and hardware applications. This function may be in the data center, in operating functional groups, or both.

In the work of managing the business information base, a security directives structure is needed as instruction for the middle and lower level managers charged with data and information infrastructure protection.

Network Security Directives
Support Information Management

Policy is a brief statement of fixed requirements and management goals. Policy requires careful reasoning and wording, as a policy should be a stable, lasting directive that tersely delivers management's instructions on what to do. A sample policy is provided later in this chapter. Implementing details (how to do it) are published in standards (or procedures, if you prefer). Standards carry the message of policy to all the employees. Reasonable, effective, and consistent application of policy requirements is achieved through publication and maintenance of current information security standards. A sample package of network security standards is offered in Chapter Six.

The information management organization functions within the security directives framework to protect business information on networks. In the end, real protection depends on the individual employees, who are gaining increasing access to the valuable business information resources. In Chapter Five we will see how to train and motivate employees to follow the security rules.

Sample Information Security Policy

Policy is the bedrock of any effort to safeguard information. The policy should be published in some form that will ensure long-term reference, such as a company policy manual. Consider the following policy against the program requirements we have just discussed.

SUMMARY

The protection of sensitive company business information is critical to continued growth and competitive effectiveness.

Certain business and technical information is classified as Business Registered, Business Confidential, or Personal. In each case, such information is to be marked accordingly. This information is to be protected through dissemination on a need-to-know basis, avoidance of careless talk, clean desk practices, limited disclosure to outside parties, and avoidance of wide distribution internally. Public disclosure of information to the press, release of financial information, and comments on legal affairs are subject to limitations specified herein.

Technical and new product information is subject to specific limitations, the most significant of which is prior approval for release.

The security of electronic information, because of its unique operational characteristics and inherent security risks, is subject to additional security provisions. These are addressed in greater detail in the Network Security Standards.

PURPOSE

This policy sets out the specific responsibilities of the corporate staff, line managers, and security coordinators.

Detailed information is provided in security standards, which are issued separately.

SCOPE

All operations of the company.

POLICY

A. Adequate safeguards will be used to protect the following information:

- Proprietary business and technical information.
- Personal data concerning applicants, employees, and former employees.
- Proprietary information of suppliers provided under contractual agreement.

B. Company Operations

- Develop organization to implement information security policy.
- Develop, publish, and implement information security plans to achieve adherence to policy.
- Initiate policies, standards, and procedures that are necessary for local requirements and legislation.
- Obtain review and concurrence of information security implementation plans by corporate security staff.
- Conduct operating unit compliance reviews.
- Identify and correct problem situations.
- Report significant information security breaches and compromises to the corporate security department.

C. Managers and Employees

- Ensure adherence to this policy and related procedures.
- Protect company classified material in accordance with established policies and procedures.
- Ensure that security indoctrination is provided to employees and contract/temporary personnel assigned to their organization.
- Designate security coordinators as required.
- Monitor implementation of information security regulations and programs.

D. Security Coordinators

- Be fully conversant with security policies and guidelines.
- Provide counsel to unit management on security matters.
- Carry out tasks and programs as set forth in the Security Coordinator Guide and perform other special assignments as required.

REFERENCES

Company Policies and Standards

CORPORATE PUBLICATIONS

Security Coordinator Guide
Personnel Manual
Information Handling Regulations Booklet
Corporate Security Handbook (Standards)

MANAGEMENT ACTION 2: GOOD SYSTEM DESIGN

System design must include both electronic and manual processes. The functional application system sponsor (or data owner) must set the value or classification of the information to be processed. The system analyst then provides controls suitable to the business application (that is, when, where, and how the information is to be used) and the data values established. These controls must ensure effective process-to-process integrity and accuracy, audit trails, and means for supervisory management and observation. The design of the system, in both automated and manual processes, must ensure that these elements of quality are maintained throughout the entire application processing cycle. In today's business environment the network is usually an integral part of most applications; security plans must address all vulnerabilities, including communications risks. For locally or individually designed systems, the designer must take into consideration potential threats to data quality from misrouting (such as use of multiple addressee lists, which might be in error) or poor collection processes; from the use of unproven software, which might contain accidental or purposeful flaws; and from design errors, which might compromise the information's validity for the intended management purposes (for instance, two people can write two programs that give correct yet different answers from processing the same data set).

Systems designers must understand the requirement for quality; to do so, they must know the value of the information and the resulting security needs of the company, the particular application, the network, and the users.

MANAGEMENT ACTION 3: EFFECTIVE
OPERATIONAL MANAGEMENT AND CONTROL

Operating management includes careful employee selection, training, and motivation; diligent design, testing, and implementation of applications and network systems; effective supervision of data collection, data center operation, local processing, and network systems operations (both locally—as for LANs—and in a macro sense) to include the company's leased long-line networks; effective supervision of employee users of network-connected workstations; disposal of obsolete or outdated information, some of which may be located in electronic files (file servers, perhaps) and not subject to normal records retention controls. Most companies have not considered the potential problems caused by an uncontrolled storing up of vast repositories of business information on electronic files, with the attendant costs and potential legal risks associated with a discovery process.

Operational management control must address a range of important matters, including clear information management policy and direction, proper systemization of work, measurement of new or changed systems against established standards in the network/systems operating environments, good direction and motivation by skilled supervisors in all work situations, and periodic, objective audits. When network-connected workstations are in use, management can never consider the control requirement to be satisfied. Business has yet to determine how to supervise knowledge workers who may create or process information at various times and places. Consider that many employees who have network access to information are professionals. Others may be clericals who do prescribed tasks on a repetitive basis with only cursory supervision. A continual effort at employee training and motivation is required. Controls are effective only if the employee is motivated to follow company practices and perceives in some sense a self-interest in doing so. I discuss means of motivation in Chapter Five.

MANAGEMENT ACTION 4:
NETWORK AND WORKSTATION SECURITY

Special measures are necessary to ensure information quality when data are handled individually by employees using network devices. Security measures are set to respond to information values or classifications and must be appropriate to the particular situation in which information is processed, transmitted, or used. Security measures consist of one or more security elements.

Security elements are found in three security element groupings or levels: physical, procedural, and logical. A combination of security elements from the three groupings can be made up to fit a particular network information security application. A successful design of a security measure for a given network situation will minimize real or perceived interference with, or complication of, the business operation. The goal is to meet protection needs in the most practical and economical manner possible, consistent with the security provided information of the same business classification in written form. Security must be a consideration throughout the network system's life cycle of design, implementation, and operation. A security measure should be designed for each operation of a system, as required, using the best possible combination of security elements appropriate to the business environment.

PART II

Planning and Implementing Network Security

THREE

Planning for Security in a Local Area Network

Management may believe that a LAN is merely another information tool. This is bad thinking. An uncontrolled LAN can be dangerous to a business, because a LAN is really a powerful information distribution and processing system, and most have many external doors, which may be open to outsiders if not purposely closed. A LAN may be as powerful as a major data processing center, but its form and content are flexible and difficult to contain. Individual employees may define the LAN's applications and interconnections, with or without management approval. The LAN presents a new kind of business world, one that requires careful planning and attention.

A NEW KIND OF NETWORK

Wide area networks, such as the ubiquitous telephone system, are planned by communications experts based on broad business communications requirements. These networks usually use public communications services, leased long lines, and value-added carriers. Any security requirements are satisfied by the addition of special hardware and software (network control systems, smart modems, encryption boxes, front-end communications controllers, and so forth) to the network circuitry. Although the designers and operators of a companywide area network may install network management and control centers and provide certain security services, the proper application of security features is almost always the responsibility of the communications service user. The managers of the network see to it that a level of service is maintained but usually accept no responsibility for the security of information on the wide area network.

Mainframe computers in data centers may be connected to the wide area network; protection for these big data base processors is usually provided in several ways. Physical protection involves the control of access to the data center and to various restricted areas inside. Logical security may be provided through an access control software package, such as ACF2 or RACF, which allow the data owners to set privileges for each authorized user based on a user profile stored on disk. Dial-up access to the mainframe computers can be controlled through the use of front-end communications processors or port control devices, often referred to as callback systems. These devices use programmed instructions to perform authentication of callers and then call back to a preset telephone number. The port control system also can limit an authorized user's activities by setting time windows, port connection authorities, and so forth.

The LAN is a different situation. Although the LAN may be connected to one or more wide area networks, and to other LANs via those networks (forming what is called an internet), the LAN is usually developed in a less formal, ad hoc manner; is a much more closely integrated system of computers and network(s) than is a wide area network; and is a new and different kind of system for most managers.

The LAN entities or servers, which provide network services, and the workstations, which act as human interfaces, are actually integral parts of the LAN. A LAN is controlled and traffic is directed by means of various clearinghouse and communications servers. Changes to or removal of any LAN device affects the characteristics of the LAN and must result in immediate changes to the network directories maintained in certain LAN devices.

In a LAN operation control of information flow and protection of information are responsibilities shared among network managers and workstation users. Network managers provide security-related services such as file backup and rely on network users to identify security requirements by setting a value for the various information items processed on the LAN. For example, users may choose to use a more secure password or to signal encryption of data by setting a flag on a certain file.

Local area networks typically cover one department, one building, or a campus of buildings. A LAN may be planned by an office manager, a single application business manager, an information systems analyst, or a data processing staff according to business application requirements. Because of the logical integration of the various workstations and servers of a LAN, security must be planned as a function of the network as an operating whole. This requires a significant management effort before the LAN is installed.

By itself, a LAN is merely a very high speed packet network. As implemented in most cases, however, the high speed of data transfer among local LAN devices allows the connection of powerful workstations with an array of special features. For example, the Xerox Network System (XNS) provides for efficient document creation, including embedded graphics, high-speed communications for both inter- and intranetwork traffic, an almost unlimited number of concurrent users, and high-volume filing services on network disk servers.

The employee who is provided with a LAN-connected workstation is getting a window to the world. Activities that would ordinarily be too tedious or difficult to consider suddenly become mundane. For example, an employee might collect software from various network-connected sources, both within and outside the company, and might store this software on-line, thus using up large amounts of costly disk space. Another person might distribute a fifty-page document electronically to five hundred people—it can be done by pushing a few keys—and thus use up a significant part of an expensive communications resource. A disgruntled employee who has been provided with privileged access to LAN controls—perhaps in a casual manner by a manager who fails to grasp the importance of such a privilege—may decide to get even by exposing or destroying key business files. Unlike volume disk files in a data center, where a miscreant must usually gain physical access, all the LAN resources may be available logically. Carelessness in planning for installation and administration of a LAN could result in a business disaster.

PLANNING A SECURE LOCAL AREA NETWORK

A number of questions must be answered before suitable security elements can be defined. Among those questions are the following:

1. What are the applications to be serviced, and what are their control and security requirements when on the LAN?
2. What business controls now in place will have to be replicated or substituted for when applications are on the LAN?
3. What protections will have to be provided for company classified information processed on the network?
4. Who are the authorized users of this network, and what security controls are appropriate to those persons or programs?
5. What network privileges are to be authorized to outsiders (nonemployees)?
6. How is high-value information to be protected?
7. What general management controls are to be established to monitor and control network activity?
8. How are problems, including security incidents, to be addressed?
9. How will local network privileges (such as rights to do system maintenance) be controlled?

Let's discuss each of these questions in turn.

What Are the Applications to Be Serviced by This LAN?

Some examples of LAN applications are:

- Message services to individuals and distribution lists.
- Calendar planning and meeting scheduling.
- Company announcements.
- Special interest groups.

- Financial analysis.
- Engineering development and coordination.
- Research and coordination.
- Publishing.
- Customer administration.
- Personnel administration.
- Real-time coordination with suppliers.
- On-line data retrieval for outside legal counsel.
- Any business functional application.

Since the LAN is, in effect, an electronic implementation of all the information functions, each application must be examined carefully to make sure that control is maintained.

Very often a LAN is installed and then applications "find their way" into the network. There is a certain benefit to this approach, as employees may discover opportunities to become more efficient by using network services. But the risk is that applications handling high-value information will be put on the network, which may not be able to provide the necessary protection. It is quite probable that this will happen, since the LAN offers such a high level of rapid information processing and communication. Strategic business files and action materials, which are natural choices for inclusion on a LAN, are the very pieces of information that should be carefully protected and strictly controlled as to distribution. Unless the network is designed to control information effectively (including while in transmission for internetworking purposes on wide area networks), management may have to choose between continuing a less efficient mode of operation and risking an exposure of critical business data.

In most cases, protection for information such as strategy data means encryption in addition to the normal levels of file access control. Many LANs do not provide encryption as a standard offering, and installation requires considerable planning and perhaps the purchase of a software package. A product called MAILSAFE, developed by RSA Data Security, implements the "public key" encryption method and appears well suited for a LAN. The package offers the ability to authenticate a message with a digital signature, thus proving its origin or authenticity. Of course, the package also provides for encryption of messages and documents. A special function allows conversion of encrypted binary files to ASCII characters for transmission if necessary.

Will Existing Business Controls Suffice?

A business activity that involves retrieval of information from central files may be an attractive candidate for a LAN application. But manual or paper-based controls may not work well in the LAN environment. Unless the LAN provides flexible controls and record keeping, the business may not be able to ensure that only proper transactions take place.

For example, in a batch processing system extensive edits can be set up because of the time lag in retrieving data or processing file updates. But in an activity using a LAN to process customer service inquiries, the network may not have facilities to make records of each inquiry and resulting action. Central files may be accessible to any of a number of employees; the network file server's or clearinghouse's control mechanism may not be able to differentiate among various employees and differing levels of employee privileges, such as read only, change, or remove. Unlike a mainframe data base application, additional controls may not be readily programmed because of the integral structure of the LAN system. Hence, other external controls may be needed.

One example of a control that may present a problem is receipting for mail. Electronic messages may provide no receipt, but a control may be required for fiscal or legal purposes. In addition, engineering applications that involve the concurrent review and change of plans and drawings may require authentication processes to identify the "original" documents in electronic form.

How Will Company Classified Information Be Handled?

Manual control processes and markings may have to be replicated in logical form on the network. A classification flag set on a file should be permanent (that is, it should stay with the file as it moves through the network) and should result in an appropriate classification marking being generated when the file is printed or displayed. The LAN also may need facilities to deal with immediate information classification decisions made when a document is created in electronic form— that is, an easy way for the workstation user to indicate the classification on the data record.

Assuming that information value decisions have been made, it must be determined how such information will be controlled and protected on the LAN. For example, if company classified documents carry a label or stamp indicating value, how will that indicator be replicated when the document is in electronic form on the LAN? One way would be to set a security bit in the header of each packet containing a classified message or document. The bit flag would then cause the creation of the appropriate label image whenever the document is displayed or printed out. Of course, a LAN workstation with graphics capabilities could be used by the originator to mark a company classified document as needed; this may not be practical, however, in some applications or for messages, which may have a telegraphic form. The provision of printer and display security marking capabilities is a matter to be addressed during network system analysis and planning.

Who Are the Authorized Users of the Network?

Unless decisions are made in the beginning about who is to be allowed to use the network, control will be lost. Individuals will share authentication, and it will be impossible to fix responsibility for unauthorized actions. Although most LANs provide for effective identification and authentication of users, the proper use of passwords or other authentication methods relies on employee motivation. This in turn requires management decisions to control access to the LAN resource.

A LAN network can be overloaded with trivial message traffic; some curious examples include a message to thousands of recipients about a study of genealogy, and another about a chocolate lover's club. Management regulations (perhaps published as standards) should provide guidance on the intended network membership. If this is not done, the net will become a huge bulletin board filled with personal notices. The issuance of an authorized password or other token is the authority to use the network. Such access must be carefully controlled. This is not to say that all employees in a certain location or job class should not have access, but that management must know who does.

Although this consideration may seem obvious, unless controls are in place from the beginning, surprising or unpleasant things may happen. LANs are like amoebas: Once operating, they seem to change form at will. Users not included in the original plans appear. Access through unplanned gateways or local, informally added communications features occurs. A formal management process is needed to control LAN facilities and users. From a security viewpoint, management must be able to identify authorized users in order to keep out all others.

What Network Privileges Are Authorized to Outsiders?

Although one may begin using a LAN with no intention of ever allowing anyone other than employees to enter the network, a perceived business advantage probably will make you want to connect suppliers, counselors, business partners, and so forth. You must clearly define how these people will use the network and how you will control their activities. In the sample security standards in Chapter Six, you will notice that outsiders are restricted to certain types of access—in that case, only through mail gateways. This restricts outsiders to sending messages; they cannot browse through network files.

To plan effectively for the kinds and complexity of access controls required, management must determine whether the LAN is to be closed (available only to employees) or open (available to anyone with access privileges). Although management will usually start out by saying that the network is just for employees, various attractive applications for connection with outsiders will come along. A few examples are:

- Connections for suppliers who may be able to cut costs by having direct access to engineering plans under development on the LAN workstations.
- Connections with outside legal counsel who may need to see current working drafts of documents concerning litigation.
- Professional groups that may be motivated to consider products favorably if

provided the courtesy of network communications facilities for certain purposes.
- Customers who want to have extended demonstration of products. Network connections could expedite customer assistance efforts or trouble analysis.

When outsiders are connected, the LAN must be prepared to set up enhanced controls and logging systems. Management should be able to set precise privileges in terms of access and actions and must be able to ascertain who is active in the net and what is going on at any given time, especially at critical network locations such as corporate headquarters. In time, all networks will probably have invited guests; it is unfair to the guests and to the company not to have effective controls in place.

How Is High-Value Information to Be Protected?

High-value information processed on a LAN requires a number of special security elements. This is so because the LAN offers so many opportunities for unauthorized access and actions. To handle high-value information safely the LAN should:

- Label all high-value documents, files, and messages with a security bit or marker to ensure that consistent protection will be provided wherever that data item may be.
- Encrypt all high-value data when they must travel over any portion of the LAN or common carrier lines through areas outside the control of the company.
- Establish an extra authentication control for access to files containing high-value data. This is intended to shut out technical staff or systems administrators who normally would have potential access by a one-time changing of passwords.
- Establish a logging mechanism to record all accesses to the high-value files, including a record of time, date, and user identity.

In addition, printers, print servers, and file servers containing or servicing high-value information should be in controlled areas, and any access to such areas should be recorded as to time, date, and individual identification (perhaps via a smart card access control system). As an alternative, a printer in a shared area could be equipped with locking bins for each user's network address.

A LAN may be perfectly suitable for most business information, but unless carefully equipped with the appropriate security software and hardware, the LAN will not be a safe place for highly sensitive business information. There is a basic conflict in any LAN between information protection and information distribution. Most LAN technologies are directed toward optimizing the user's access to information throughout the network. Security managers, of course, are interested in limiting access to data the employee needs to know. In some cases, authorized users who need to exchange information find that LAN naming or addressing schemes make interconnection difficult. These people may use wild card file addresses (in XNS, an asterisk), thus allowing anyone to access their files. This is convenient but extremely risky.

What General Management Controls Should Be Used to Monitor and Control Network Activity?

When LANs were first introduced, many users thought they could merely install the hardware and the network would take care of itself. They were wrong. Local area networks are particularly demanding of management. They are powerful, complex, distributed, flexible information systems. Carefully planned, well-structured management controls are required for effective, secure operation, which will ensure quality business information.

Management controls should include procedures for the following:

- Managing conformance with company network standards of operation.
- Controlling the network environment; this refers to any changes or modifications of the internet or LAN services, topography, or infrastructure.
- Defining and monitoring network operations services and support services. This requirement reflects the integrated nature of a LAN; if a local service is withdrawn or inoperative, it can affect other services and other connected LANs, perhaps by delaying delivery of messages.
- Defining service levels expected, including security services, so that a dependable and consistent level of network service is provided at all workstations. For example, is a clearinghouse server expected to be operative seven days a week?
- Resolving network problems, including a process for escalation of technical problems and eventual reporting to the supplier of the LAN equipment or software.
- Establishing network configuration management, including determining how additional nodes or services are to be added in a controlled manner within the overall capacity of the network given a target service level. This is critical, since very often the LAN technology allows unlimited additional units to be added by merely connecting an adapter to the LAN cable. Unlimited additions to the network can severely compromise service levels; more importantly, unidentified users are a security risk.
- Creating a controlled procedure for implementing upgrades to equipment or installing new software releases. Since a LAN or interconnected series of LANs form an integrated whole, changes must be made only after careful planning and with control. Careless changes to LAN environments could result in the placement of Trojan horse software or the compromise of information integrity or privacy during time periods when control may be lost.
- Settling a management structure similar to that for providing telecommunica-

tions services. In some companies this can be the same organization. This group operates the wide area network control centers and manages the servicing and maintenance of both the wide area and local area networks. Security is very difficult to establish if no one is responsible for general network services.

How Are Problems, Including Security Incidents, to Be Handled?

A process of reporting incidents and problems through succeedingly higher levels of organization must be established to ensure correction or investigation as appropriate. Most security incidents require a dual reporting activity; that is, a report must go through network management channels, and the same report must go through organizational security channels. The incident may threaten both the integrity of the network and the information involved.

The users of a LAN probably report to different people in the organization and seldom to the LAN manager; reporting of problems may be inconsistent and ineffectual unless a formal process for handling troubles is established. Security incidents should be promptly reported to the local security manager; delays can compromise effective investigation. Appendix C shows a problem resolution procedure for a LAN internet.

How Will Local Network Privileges Be Managed?

Certain people may require special authorization. These include maintenance people, systems administrators, and managers. In a situation where individual LANs are interconnected, or where office LANs are clustered on a site, different management approaches may be required to control the granting of privileges. In an office network or for a local, campus cluster of LANs, local management must have the responsibility for authorizing the granting of special privileges. Examples of special privileges are those given to systems administrators, who set up new LAN accounts or delete accounts and handle problems, and to systems maintenance engineers, who require special access. A formal procedure should be set up so that the granting of any local privilege, even those temporarily given in case of absence, is documented and approved by a responsible manager. For the sake of controlling access to sensitive information and for preserving the integrity of the network, privileges should be held to the absolute minimum. Our sample network security standards set the limit at two persons with privileges per LAN.

Summary

Effective security requires careful analysis and planning. Local area networks are often installed without sufficient work analysis and planning. This is unfortunate because maximum benefits are realized only when the network system is designed to meet rational business needs. As in the case of business applications, little is gained by automating a bad procedure. The security manager has an important role to play in designing an application of a LAN; this role involves identification of information values and security requirements during the network planning process and evaluation of network operations after installation. These responsibilities are covered in detail in an earlier book (Schweitzer 1983).

Careful attention to LAN security requirements during the planning process should ensure that, when the LAN is installed and running, business users will be able to develop applications without fear that unacceptable risks will be taken. A LAN that cannot handle the company's high-value information is a crippled network.

RISK AND COUNTERMEASURES ANALYSIS

Many managers prefer to have all business alternatives quantified to support decisions to expend resources. For network security, such quantification requires a formal risk analysis. This can be done manually, using a good dose of common sense, or automatically with any of a number of software packages now available. Doing a LAN risk analysis is worthwhile during the planning stage and at regular intervals (every three years?) thereafter.

Charles Cresson Wood (1986) says there are four primary methods used to evaluate risks in information systems operations. These are:

1. Checklists that describe specific control measures, with provisions for indicating whether or not the protection is provided. The individual items on the list may be weighted. Checklists are helpful in getting a picture of serious shortcomings, but one must take care not to accept a checklist item as being a general requirement. Checklists do not provide an acceptable risk evaluation process.
2. Quantitative risk analysis provides an implicit or explicit decision-making process supporting spending on security. It is a formal and structured approach in which threats are described and weighted, usually with monetary values based on information assets at risk. The cost of proposed controls may then be matched with the risk values. This approach is well suited to computer applications. Probability theory is used. One serious flaw is that the various pieces of data applied to the computation are all guesses of one sort or another; we do not have enough experience to construct tables such as the mortality tables used by life insurance companies.
3. Scenario construction develops threat occurrence stories involving people, processing infrastructure, and communications. Controls required to stop such scenarios from developing are identified and matched against current controls.
4. Information flow tracing is used extensively by auditors and follows the

movement of a piece of information throughout a business process life cycle. Controls are evaluated at each step based on the value and importance of the information.

Performing a risk analysis usually involves a number of steps:

- Application vulnerabilities must be identified so that management is aware of where, when, and how a threat might be realized.
- The probability that an event will occur needs to be set; this is necessarily an estimate, usually in times per year.
- Potential losses, should a threat materialize, must be estimated. Cost data usually are developed by order of magnitude—that is, the loss would be $100, $1,000, $10,000, $100,000, and so forth.
- Security protection elements to guard against the threat must be identified and costed.
- The rate of return on the security investment must be set; without it, one cannot decide whether the security investment is worthwhile. In many cases, business should just accept the risk.

Most risk analysis ends up with a process that goes something like this:

(probability of threat occurring) × (cost of occurrence) = risk value

It is evident that the accuracy of the result depends on the quality of the estimates used. As your risk analysis encompasses wider areas of business operations, the quality of these estimates seriously deteriorates. For one application, the results may be meaningful. For a large, interconnected network, results must be questioned. It is best to do one LAN at a time.

Some risk analysis systems are available from:

Profile Analysis Corporation
PO Box 875
454 Main Street
Ridgefield, CT 06877

International Security Technology
11250 Roger Bacon Drive, Suite 11
Reston, VA 22090

FOUR

Selecting Appropriate Security Elements

Communications networks that connect computers and workstations are essential if businesses are to realize maximum benefits from the investment in computing resources. And yet networks represent the most severe information control and security challenge. Briefly, the problem is to make information widely available to those who need it, while ensuring that the information retains the quality attributes of reliability, integrity, and privacy.

Over the past twenty years, the computer has brought about major changes in the way information is handled in business. Today, most organizations have several large mainframe computers, often located in multiple data centers. These large, data base–supporting processors are interconnected by one or more networks using the variety of networking technologies now available. The central processors probably include a number of different machine architectures, each designed to optimize results for a given set of applications. The networks connecting this mix of machines and operating systems allow individual employees to share data from the information bases of the company and to perform local computer processes using personal computers or workstations. In addition, LANs provide integrated workstations and services on campuses, within buildings, and for functional departments.

There may be hundreds or thousands of workstation or personal computer users interconnected with the mix of central processors, LAN servers, and each other. The personal computer/workstation user connected to these networks is, in effect, a data center manager as far as information security is concerned. He or she can retrieve data, process the data through untested application programs, and send the resulting information to any network address. By using the computing power in a personal computer the user may be able to modify local access privileges and possibly bypass existing local controls.

A NETWORK IS NOT A DATA CENTER

The kinds, variety, and severity of security vulnerabilities found in networked microcomputers are markedly different from those encountered in data centers

49

or time-sharing applications, where a number of terminal devices are connected to a central mainframe. From a security viewpoint the important differences are:

	Data Center	*Distributed Network*
Environment	Constrained to identified user group tied to applications	Potentially open via internetwork connections
Information base	Defined and controlled	Undefined; control relies on users
Information flow	Point to point	Unrestricted
Physical access control	Critical to data base infrastructure	Of relatively minor importance since data is distributed
Logical access control	Protects files	Protects files and network integrity

In contrast to the traditional physical and logical controls implemented at one place, which are typical of a data center security scheme, a network of computers, workstations, and other devices requires these information security measures:

1. Control of access to all information files accessible from the home network or from connected foreign networks.
2. Control of activity once authorized entry to a file has been allowed.
3. Control of access to network traffic.
4. Establishment of effective identification and authentication means for each network user, human and logical, and for each network component.
5. Control of access to network resources (including clearinghouses, communications controllers, front ends, and various servers), physically and logically, both from home domains (such as hard-wired or directly connected devices) and from foreign locations (such as a dial-in from any telephone or penetration via internetwork connections).
6. Control of information propagation to prevent distribution or leaking to unauthorized network stations or users.

Table 4.1 shows the various risks and security elements applicable to each risk.

Rutledge and Hoffman (1986) suggest a model for network security that mathematically expresses the relationship of the various security elements:

$$S = f(P1*P2*A*C1*C2)$$

where S is total system security, P1 is physical security, P2 is personnel security (trustworthiness and awareness), A is administrative controls, C1 is data communications security, and C2 is computer processing security. Rutledge and Hoffman consider each element in the equation to be valued between 0 (lack of security) and 1 (complete security). Using the formula with "fuzzy logic" to evalu-

Table 4.1 Risks v. Security Elements

Risks	Applicable Security Elements		
	Physical	Logical	Procedural
Unauthorized access to information on network files	File servers secured	Access control system; encryption logging	Authorization process
Eavesdropping by: wiretap emanations		Encryption Shielding of VDUs	
Activity at file: unauthorized authorized but improper		Access control Logging; control granularity	
Improper distribution of information		Software constraints tied to value flags	Administrative control of use of lists
Improper use of privileged access	Network facilities secured	Logging; granularity of process	Limited authority
Physical attack on network components	Network facilities secured		

ate the effectiveness of each element in the business situation can provide a form of risk assessment for a network (Schmucker 1983). Very good protection would fall into the 0.8 to 0.9 range, while anything less than 0.3 would be suspect. Such a risk assessment might be useful at this stage.

We are using the Xerox Network System (XNS) as a model. While the security elements we identify here are generally applicable to all types of LANs, we should recognize that the various systems have differing risk and protection outlines. Britain's National Computing Centre offers some interesting comparisons in its excellent booklet *Office Systems Security* (Ellison and Pritchard 1986). These comparisons are shown in relation to the transmission media, the network technology, the transmission technique and the access and sharing technique, as shown in Tables 4.2 through 4.4.

DETAILS OF IMPLEMENTATION

Controlling Access to Connected Information Files

Controlling access to information files is the crux of the security problem. One cannot reasonably expect to keep all unwanted or unauthorized people out of the

Table 4.2   Network Topologies and Relative Security

Topology	Security Strengths	Security Weaknesses	Comments
Star (central node employs switching to connect peripheral nodes)	Easy to attach new devices without distributing the system Central node can provide circuit, message, or packet switching	Central node fails, then the whole system crashes Central node therefore needs good physical and logical security Dedicated point-to-point corrections; no broadcast facility available	Central node contains intelligence, therefore cheap peripheral nodes Readily available in the form of PABX
Loop (all messages routed through an intelligent controller)	Broadcast facility available (useful to remind users to change their password, for example)	Loop controller fails, then system fails; need good physical and logical security for this controller Low-speed transmission restricts throughput	Control node contains intelligence, hence a cheap peripheral node
Ring (each node has equal amount of intelligence)	No central node with its associated security problems Ring monitor station monitors performance and can remove corrupted packets (i.e., easy to control) Every node gets an equal chance to transmit	Break in the ring, stops the system (some proprietary systems are reconfigurable) Must take the whole system down to add a new node	More intelligence required in each node; nodes are therefore relatively more expensive
Bus or highway (peripherals hang onto the bus waiting for their packets)	No central node A break in the bus, isolating one device, may not affect the whole system (depends on system) Easily expandable	Data throughput may degrade under heavy usage Some systems may need a manual clock	More intelligence required in each node; nodes are therefore relatively more expensive

Reprinted by permission of The National Computing Centre, Ltd., from "Security in Office Systems."

Table 4.3 Access or Sharing on LANs: Security Characteristics

Access or Sharing Technique	Advantages	Disadvantages	Comments
Token passing	Every node gets a fair chance to transmit No limit to packet size	Detection of lost/ corrupt packets is essential Fairly complex to implement	Not suitable for real-time applications
Carrier sense multiple access with collision detection (CSMA/CD)	Makes good use of medium Good for "bursty" traffic Transmitter can hear if a collision is happening Can be up to 90 percent efficient	Performance falls with high utilization Access times cannot be guaranteed No use for synchronous data transmission, voice traffic, video	Most common technique Basis of Ethernet
Carrier series multiple access with collision avoidance (CSMA/CA)	Best for when some nodes need more access to the system and where the overall loading is fairly high	Devices on the network need to have a reasonable amount of intelligence More expensive than other systems	Combination of TDM and CSMA/CD
Fixed slot	As TDM	As TDM	Used in ring system
Empty slot	Nodes have a fair share of bandwidth Performs well under heavy loads Monitors spots and removes defective packets	Reliability can be a problem, as it depends on monitor, repeater, and using segments Needs a monitor station	Cambridge ring is one example
Frequency division multiplexing (FDM)	Bandwidth can be split up into a number of dedicated channels Hardware is readily available	Channels require guard bands to minimize the effects of crosstalk Modems must be used at the appropriate channel frequency	Overall bandwidth is limited by the bandwidth at the worst component
Time division multiplexing (TDM)	Each device has a preallocated time slot Economical	Channel capacity can be wasted	Not suitable for real-time applications

(*continued*)

Table 4.3 *(continued)*

Access or Sharing Technique	Advantages	Disadvantages	Comments
Polling	Each device can have exclusive use of the controller	Only really applicable to low-usage terminals	Used especially in star networks Not suitable for real-time applications
Broadcast bus	Used packet formatting allows for easy detection and correction of erroneous information (trailer contains a field check sequence, which is examined by the receiving node to see if it has been damaged in transit) Very efficient	Only one user can send information at a time	User packets have header, trailer, and message blocks

Reprinted by permission of The National Computing Centre, Ltd., from "Security in Office Systems."

network infrastructure. There are just too many interconnections with uncontrollable environments (such as the communications utility's switching centers, other connected networks, and dial-up services). The essential security measure is a selective access control at the point where information can be had. Control of access to files means that the security system must be able to authenticate users, then determine which information elements each authenticated user is authorized to have. Such a system presupposes that the information owner has made decisions about information values and has been able to specify who may see or operate on the information. (Here we see that information security is a part of the general process called *information resource management.*)

Access to files is usually controlled through a user profile, which describes the individual user in terms of the information privileges associated with his or her job. When the user authenticates a claimed identity to the control system by using a token (for instance, a password, a physical identifier such as a fingerprint, or a plastic card), the system determines the user's information access rights by referring to an established rights table. A second method is to provide each user with a password or other means to unlock individual file controls. This approach

Table 4.4 LAN Transmission Media and Security Characteristics

Transmission Media	Security Strengths	Security Weaknesses	Comments
Optical fiber	Signals do not radiate outside the medium, hence secure from eavesdroppers Secure from external electromagnetic interference Physically small Very low loss	Tapping the fiber to add new devices is difficult Dispersion effects can be a problem	Relatively expensive Suited to ring and loop networks
Twisted pair cable	Tried and tested Easy to install Transmits digital and analog information	Radiates to environment when transmitting data, therefore needs shielding to be secure from eavesdroppers Not easy to add a new device Cannot be used in electrically noisy environments unless shielded (high attenuation of signal)	Readily available Best for point-to-point links Low cost
Multiway cable	Tried and tested Easy to install Control and data lines can be split, making interfacing very easy; parallel data transmission possible	Radiates to environment when transmitting data, therefore needs shielding to secure from eavesdroppers Cannot be used in electrically noisy environments	Readily available Best for baseband ring or bus systems More expensive than either twisted pair or coaxial
Coaxial cable	Shielded and secure from external electromagnetic interference Signals do not radiate outside the cable (except baseband) Tried and tested Easy to connect new devices	Ease of tapping the line to connect new devices can be a security threat Baseband usage makes eavesdropping possible	Readily available Available as baseband or broadband Ideal for broadcast network High bit rate transmission possible Better quality cable; can be expensive for broadband

Reprinted by permission of The National Computing Centre, Ltd., from "Security in Office Systems."

has a number of deficiencies and is seldom used outside of local, personal computing where individuals may set passwords to protect private files on a desktop microcomputer.

A number of authentication systems designed for network use are now providing interfaces for mainframe software packages such as ACF2. In these systems, the user typically has a hand-held key or signal generator, which validates a signal from a coordinated processor at a central site. These systems allow the user profile at the central processor to be coordinated with the individual network authentication process. Table 4.5 shows some network control products available in 1987.

What to Do

- Understand the user authentication process provided by the manufacturer of your company's LAN; most security systems allow some latitude in application. Select the method that best suits your company's operation and information value but ensures that network management can maintain control.
- Insist that each user have a unique personal identifier. Do not allow users to share authentication tokens for any reason. Remember, it is important to be able to fix responsibility for actions if the company wishes to maintain control over network resources. (See below: Establishing Effective Identification and Authentication.)

Controlling Activity at the File Level

Once connected, the user must be restricted as to what he or she may do. This restriction relates to the individual's job assignment. For example, a personnel administrator may be allowed to access the payroll records of all employees in a certain unit. But the personnel administrator is probably not allowed to make changes to the wage records. This sort of control is based on rights such as read only, move, change, and so forth, usually established as part of the file level controls and triggered by the user's personal identifier.

In a LAN environment, in contrast to a single computer–terminal connection, such activity restrictions are critical, since there is a greater potential that an unauthorized party may be able to find a path to the file.

What to Do

- Make sure the data owner of each file has established activity rights for each user or class of user authorized access. This is especially important when the information is of high value.
- Make sure that authorized activity privileges are current with business operations needs. One way to do this is to periodically have the data owner sign off on the privileges table. This should be done at least annually for each LAN file server.

Table 4.5 Combination Dial-Up Security Systems Available in January 1987

Vendor/Product	Description	Price
Atalla/Confidante (408) 435-8850	For IBM MVS/TSO host software; smart card	$15,000 (software); $35 to $95 (card)
Codercard/Codercard (714) 833-3053	Unit at asynchronous host; smart card; encryption options	$450 (unit); $55 (card)
Datakey/Netlock (612) 890-6850	Unit at asynchronous host; smart card	$600 to $1,000
Digital Pathways/Defender IID with Securenet Key (415) 964-0707	Unit at host; smart card; encryption options available	$4,100 to $7,000 (unit); $50 (card)
Enigma Logic/Safeword Systems (415) 827-5707	Software for IBM MVS/TSO, DEC VAX, or Unix hosts; smart card; decoder	$2,500 and up (software); $65 to $75 (decoder and card)
Gordian System/Gordian Access Management Systems (415) 494-8414	Host software; smart card	$25,000
Leemah Datacom Security/Traqnet with Safetraq (415) 786-0790	Unit at host; smart card; decoder	$995 (unit); $275 (card and decoder)
Mastiff System/Mastiff Terminal Protection (404) 984-0202	Hand-held key unit; loop antenna at host	$250 and up
Microframe/Datalock 4000 (609) 395-7800	Unit at host; hand-held key unit; encryption options available	$3,500 (unit); $120 to $500 (card)
Optimum Electronics/DL 1000 and DL Access Key (203) 239-6098	Unit at host; smart card	$2,625 (unit); $250 (card)
Secure Data Assoc./Caps-1 (801) 263-1661	Unit at host; hand-held card; data access terminal	$1,995 (unit); $500 (terminal); $100 (card)
Security Dynamics/ACE System with SecurID (617) 547-7820	Unit at host; host software for DEC VAX under VMS or Ultrix; hand-held key device	$22,500 and up (software); $6,800 (unit); $34 (card)
Sytek/PFX Passport (415) 966-7300	Software for IBM PC–based server; authentication card	$5,000 to $10,000 (software); $75 to $110 (card)
United Software Security/Lazerlock System (703) 556-0007	Host software (e.g., ACF2) for IBM mainframes under MVS; micro-based encryption software; hand-held card	$33,000 (ACF2); $6,500 (Padpath); $2,250 (encryption software); $75 (card)

Controlling Activity at the Record Level

Within a file written on a disk at the LAN file server, we may find various record sets. A record is a collection of data. In the XNS, our model in this book, records are stored as file folders or documents. The basic record is a document, which relates to a paper document. It may have one or several pages of data, arranged as text, tables, graphics, or a combination thereof. One or more documents may be stored in a file folder. Users can reference a file folder by subject using display icons, then search through the folder for a certain document.

For minimal security purposes, we would want to be able to restrict access to file drawers, as we can in a physical office process. It would be desirable, recognizing the power of electronics, if we also could specify authorization to access file folders. Thus, a logical file drawer could be specified for public access, but by setting restrictions based on user authentication at the clearinghouse, we could deny access to specific folders or documents. In many businesses this is highly desirable. Consider the documents in a legal firm or a personnel department, where only specific people are supposed to see individual documents. The ability to restrict access at a level lower than a file is a security plus.

Controlling Access to Network Traffic

For high-value or sensitive information, it is important that casual observers or intentional wiretappers not be able to observe network traffic. In some cases, information privacy can be violated through network traffic analysis. For example, a skilled analyst may be able to determine a pending strategic business move by observing the numbers and addresses of messages, without actually knowing the contents of the messages. Such a case might involve bank transfers. When high-value information is passed over a network, an eavesdropper can gain important data, just by seeing traffic passing by.

In such cases where network traffic must be protected, encryption is the only effective means of security. Encrypted information is a data stream that has been encoded by passing it through a complex algorithm producing a nonrepetitive cypher. Encryption usually is performed automatically by computer hardware processes. In some instances, encryption can be called as a software-based service routine.

Most encryption systems today are based on the Data Encryption Standard published by the U.S. Bureau of Standards. A more promising technique for network applications is the public key encryption system (Rivest, Shamir, and Adelman 1977). The public key system uses the properties of large prime numbers to allow each user to publish a key, then decrypt or decode incoming messages with a second, secret key. Among the advantages of such a system are the ability to "sign" a message (that is, to prove the identity of the originator or the genuineness of the text) and the elimination of onerous key distribution requirements. A commercial electronic mail version of the system is now available from RSA Data Security Inc. of Redwood City, California.

What to Do

- Understand the encryption process available on your LAN or install encryption software or equipment.
- Determine the high-value/high-risk situations in the operation of company networks. Apply encryption sparingly as required. (An occasional high-value business message may be considered secure if mixed among other traffic; if frequent high-value messages occur on a link, encrypt that link.)

Establishing Effective Identification and Authentication

Effective information management requires that we be able to identify each network entity that may access or process information. Entities may be persons or network facilities such as file servers, printers, and central processors. Identification consists of a unique name or code for each entity. For humans, this could be a real name, an alias, an employee number, or any other unique form. For nonhuman entities, the identifier can be an assigned name or code. The critical requirement is that each identifier be unique. This poses some real problems in a large business with thousands of connected workstations and hundreds of data base computers. Many real and assumed names or codes will turn out to be redundant. There must be another way.

One solution is through compartmentalized identifiers that use a hierarchical approach. Consider a network name that consists of three parts: entity, division (or other organizational level), and country. A user name might be "John Smith/Manufacturing/Canada." Of course, the parts could be abbreviated: JSmith/Man/Can, as long as a replication of an abbreviation for another division or country does not occur. Notice that this is a far more complex problem than the traditional identifier used for access to a single, stand-alone computer. With the potential for perhaps 100,000 names and 10,000 locations, and with the potential for hundreds of J.Smiths, ensuring unique identifiers requires planning. The same approach can be used for nonhuman entities—for example, using the same organization and country: "Print server 2/Manufacturing/Canada" or, PS2/Man/Can. This type of identifier allows fast, efficient identification and location; it is similar to a network addressing scheme. In many cases, the two are synonymous.

Authentication refers to the proving of a claimed identity. Although a password is the most typical authentication token, it has many weaknesses. Stronger authentication involves the use of physical characteristics or biometrics—fingerprints, voiceprints, eye retina scans—which cannot be altered and are reliably unique. Also better are answer-back systems, which rely on the user's knowing a formula, and physical tokens, such as pocket-size code generators, which coordinate with a network security center.

The use of authentication tokens other than, or in addition to, passwords involves adding system components, usually combinations of software and hardware, to allow the token to interface with the system. The hand-held password generator responds to a signal from a terminal device generated by a central processor, and an entry on the keyboard. Obviously, the system must use either programmed instructions or added circuit boards to provide the necessary services. Because of the costs involved (and because computer manufacturers still do not provide built-in security), most network systems continue to use the password as authenticator.

If passwords are used, we must convince users to practice good password discipline. Almost all the unauthorized penetrations of network-connected computer systems to date have resulted from carelessness in system design or implementation, including user errors or disregard for password discipline. To be reasonably effective, passwords should be at least six characters in length, not easily guessed but relevant to the user, and changed at least twice each year. The longer a password, the more difficulty a would-be penetrator will have in obtaining it, whether by guess or by computation.

Lance J. Hoffman, in his book *Modern Methods for Computer Security and Privacy,* discusses the effects of password length and provides a formula for developing passwords that create a desired *work factor* (the time or cost needed to obtain a password). Very simply, Hoffman proves that the construction of the password directly affects its *safetime,* or that time for which a user may feel secure from an attacker who is trying to guess (or compute) a password. As an example, Hoffman says that increasing the length of a password by just one character significantly increases the safetime: If the expected safetime of a three-character password is three months (as computed from the formula), the safetime for a four-character password is seventy-eight months (Hoffman 1977).

The form of the password is also important. The user should be able to remember it with certainty (and thus not feel constrained to write it down), but it also should be very difficult for others to guess. The telephone number of a high school sweetheart or a street address from long ago are examples of forms meeting the criteria.

Controlling Access to Network Infrastructure Resources

So far we have dealt with the logical or electronic access to a system, but one must also be concerned about physical access to the network infrastructure. This includes the switching centers, data centers, network servers, and communication junction boxes. All LAN resources should be considered privileged; that is, as a general rule casual users should never be allowed to have access to, or manipulate, LAN servers. Effective office physical access controls are a minimal requirement. Rooms containing network control units, such as clearinghouses, communication servers, and file servers, should be strictly controlled and monitored. Access should be limited to those persons formally identified by local network managers.

Network administrators or systems administrators require privileged access to network resources for maintenance purposes. These privileges should be definable at a level that permits precise control of who may do what. For example, a systems administrator should be limited to those privileges necessary to perform assigned tasks and no more. The systems administrator responsible for backing up files, for example, has no need for privileged access to clearinghouse or communication services on the LAN. When high-value files are in file servers, only specifically authorized persons should be given privileged access to those files; in addition, such privileges should be qualified so that the person holding the privilege may do only necessary maintenance work and not change the data.

Although not strictly a part of the network, on-line printers also must be secured. An encrypted message that is printed out in clear text and allowed to sit in a printer output bin is vulnerable to casual observation. The cost and discipline of the logical parts of the system are for naught if casual passers-by can look at sensitive information that has otherwise been controlled. Using locking bins or password-controlled print queues is recommended.

In some LANs knowledgeable persons with physical access to network clearinghouses could change an authenticator and thus be able to impersonate a valid user, with access to that user's protected files. A logical corollary to this is the changing of job responsibilities of employees who have network security privileges, such as systems administrators. Care must be taken to cancel physical access rights and logical authentication when an employee moves to another job or leaves the company.

The necessary physical protection measures should be obvious: Keep anyone not authorized to have information away from the network infrastructure and its component parts. In most cases this involves locking rooms or otherwise controlling access to the spaces in which network-connected machines are located.

What to Do

- Plan network support facilities with security and serviceability in mind. A LAN cannot simply be added like a typewriter or video screen. A significant support structure, in terms of human resources and access-controllable facilities spaces, is required.

Logical access to network devices also is important. Such access may be from within the network itself—by authorized network users or by others—or via dial-up connections. Improper connections with network servers or controllers from user terminal devices have the potential for seriously damaging LAN serviceability and reliability. To eliminate this threat, clearinghouse algorithms or tables used for routing mail could be changed. Unauthorized access to network facilities could allow copying of network traffic, insertion of false data, or interference with messages. Strict network configuration policies are needed to control the kinds of external access connections allowed. In general, any connection from outside the business network should be restricted as to activities and destinations allowed.

Protecting Against Unauthorized Connections from Telephone Links

The public telephone network offers a ready, convenient, and cheap way for unauthorized persons to attempt to gain access to computers and computer networks. All that is needed is a terminal device, a modem, and, of course, a telephone. Most LANs offer dial-in connections for convenience; in the XNS, such a connection is made via a service called ITS.

Protection against unauthorized callers gaining access to a computer, and hence the network, depends on some kind of port control device. These are often referred to as callback devices, reflecting one of their features. The U.S. Bureau of Standards identifies six types of port control hardware (U.S. Bureau of Standards 1986).

Single-end devices provide a control at the computer/network end of the connection only. These include:

1. Host port protection devices, fitted between the host computer and the modem or between the modem and the telephone set. They provide for a table of passwords and can hide or camouflage the host by presenting a unique screen display or answer so that the caller cannot ascertain whether a computer is present on the line. These devices can signal to operators when an attack is made. They do not call back.
2. Security modems, controlled by passwords, which are really extra-capability modems equipped with solid-state devices to perform callback when a user password is entered.

Double-end devices, where a hardware unit is placed at both the caller and host (network) ends of the line, include:

1. Token identification systems, where the caller must present a hardware key or small device to generate an authentication code, thus completing a connection.
2. Terminal authentication devices, which use a device mounted on the terminal

or inserted in-line at the terminal to authenticate that device to the host. This authentication can be used to limit a user to certain actions or terminals.

3. Line encryption devices, which prevent unauthorized traffic, and hence access, because the unauthorized caller does not have the necessary key to send valid data forms.

4. Message and data authentication devices, usually found in electronic funds transfer systems, which apply a crytographic check-sum approach requiring the caller and recipient to authenticate each other.

The use of port control devices is really a supplement to the other levels of security already mentioned in this chapter. Basic network and file controls must be in place and properly administered. When a risk from dial-in traffic is perceived (almost always the case when dial-in is permitted), a port control device is appropriate. It should be selected after careful analysis of the situation and consideration of the various products available. (For a useful review see U.S. Bureau of Standards 1986).

What to Do

- Establish how the network is to be administered. Most applications of LANs in business will require dedicated administrative service people to maintain access controls, establish user accounts, provide file backup, and so forth.
- Limit the number of people who will be given special privileges on the network. Establish management controls over such authorizations.
- Establish privilege at a fine enough level so that real control may be established. One system administrator should never be able to perform all actions; responsibilities should be parceled out. Critical tasks should be shared so that a collusion is necessary to attack high-value files.
- Determine whether a port control device will be useful in the situation.
- Prepare for emergency situations when the usual network service people may not be available.

Controlling Information Propagation and Leakage

The power of modern networks, and the reason we use them to get the most benefit from our investment in computer resources, is the ability to move information about swiftly. This potential for information transfer also presents us with a security challenge. Information on networks, whether retrieved from a data base or sent as electronic mail, can easily get out of control. It can end up in the wrong person's mailbox, or it can be assembled from apparently harmless bits of data into critically damaging information summaries that reveal product plans, market strategies, or business plans.

There are three ways in which information leakage can occur. First, information can be left unprotected at various places in the network(s), allowing the curious browser, intentional penetrator, or industrial espionage agent to collect intelligence. Even with a relatively low level of access authority, users may be able to poke around in the thousands of network places containing information. In some cases, poorly motivated users may accumulate information in files that are available to all network users or to large classes of users. Eventually, such blanket authorizations are a severe risk, as significant intelligence may be accumulated in files unintentionally and may then be available to persons with no need to know, or who may seek opportunities for improper or illegal activity.

Second, destination addresses can be given in error, resulting in information being delivered to the wrong party. Even worse, since the actual recipients are relatively invisible, is the use of distribution lists. Information sent to distribution lists may be exposed because the wrong list is used or because the list used contains network entities not authorized to have the information. In many cases, LAN users do not have assurance that the members of a distribution list are as assumed; some members may be outside the network, or even outside the company. Some LANs provide mail-forwarding features; an employee who moves to another company that also has a LAN, perhaps connected with ARPANET or another semipublic network, may be able to direct future messages to a new network address at another location or within another company. If the person is on network distribution lists, data may be sent outside the company unknowingly for an extended period of time.

Third, weak management controls may allow unidentified entities to use the network. An example would be so-called guest accounts used for demonstration or other purposes. If business purposes justify the use of the LAN by outsiders, the company should have established effective authorization and identification controls for such cases. For example, the guest identifier should clearly indicate a sponsor, perhaps as follows: "Guest/Sponsor:Domain:Network."

What to Do

- Establish procedures for the distribution of high-value information. Generally, distribution lists should not be used.
- Require that every user be identified as a human being; in other words, make certain that every single action on the network can be traced to a responsible employee. Never use function or location names for accounts, even if those accounts are for purely administrative purposes.

ENCRYPTION: THE ULTIMATE PROTECTION

Encryption—the coding of information using a nonrepetitive cypher—provides the strongest security possible for information being transmitted on networks or stored on disks or tapes. But encryption is expensive and requires great care in its use, so the decision to encrypt should not be taken lightly.

Background

Information has been coded throughout history to protect it from those who were not supposed to have it. In Rome Caesar is supposed to have used a form of encryption—the simple Caesar cypher—to hide secret plans for military movements. In World War II the U.S. military broke the Japanese code, thus allowing a tremendous advantage in the naval strategy for the Pacific theater of operations. Today sophisticated encryption schemes are no doubt a part of every advanced nation's diplomatic and military communications systems. And encryption forms the basis for the control and security of most modern network schemes (Needham and Schroeder 1978). The authentication of network users to network control centers and clearinghouses requires nonforgeable proof, and encryption provides that proof. Encryption is essential to the secure operation of any network.

The term *encryption* refers to the coding of information using a cryptographic scheme. Technically, we should use the term *cryptography,* which means encoding; *decryption* means decoding. But encryption has become the commonly accepted term, so I will use it throughout this chapter.

One can encrypt data manually—that is, by using pencil and paper. The Captain Midnight code rings that millions of children ordered through the mail during the 1940s and 1950s were an example of a simple encoding device. Computers, of course, can do a much better job. We would not want to use a simple cypher because people would quickly determine the code and we would not protect our information. The most basic cypher merely substitutes a 1 for an *a,* a 2 for a *b,* and so forth. To be secure, we must have a nonrepetitive substitution based on a random selection of code. This is necessary so that an analyst cannot determine our code by checking for the most frequently used character, which in English would most likely represent *e.*

Current encryption systems use a mathematical process called an algorithm to produce a cypher or substitution that is very difficult to decode without the encryption key. The key is a number, or seed, that when entered in the algorithm, causes the coded information to be produced in a form that can later be decyphered by reentering that same key.

Two general types of encryption systems are in use today for commercial purposes. The first is represented by the various proprietary systems produced by the manufacturers or developers of encryption software and hardware packages. It includes the Data Encryption Standard, or DES system, developed by IBM and the U.S. Bureau of Standards. The second type is the public key system developed by some researchers at the Massachusetts Institute of Technology (MIT).

DES Encryption Systems

Cryptography is a complex science; I will not go into detail in this book because the security or business manager need not understand the mathematical aspects of encryption. If more detail is desired, an excellent description is provided by Lance Hoffman in his chapter titled "Privacy Transformations" (Hoffman 1977).

The DES type of encryption system can be implemented in hardware or software. Hardware systems are usually preferred because software-based encryption tends to impose a high overhead, or delay, on computer processing. DES systems and similar, proprietary encryption methods use an algorithm (formula) to process plaintext into ciphertext, or code. The key, typically a large number, is entered into the encryption system before encryption takes place. Generally, the more complex the key, the more difficult the solution. Once encrypted, there is no way to recover the information without the key. This means that management of the encryption keys is very important.

With the computer as the encryption machine, replacing pencil and paper or mechanical devices such as the German enigma machine of World War II, the modern cryptographer is not concerned with finding a complex key to confuse would-be code breakers. Rather he or she tries to develop an algorithm that defies solution, even if the expert attempting to decipher the coded text should have plenty of enciphered text to work with.

The computer allows a number of substitutions and transpositions using circuits arranged in sets, called permutation boxes. Picture a box in which eight wires enter, are crossed over and among one another, and then come out the other side in a confused order. The DES algorithm is a logical implementation of a series of such boxes arranged in different groups.

Handling Encryption Keys

Encryption has been used for a long time. Traditionally, messengers delivered the appropriate keys to those who were authorized to decode messages. Obviously, this method was vulnerable to a variety of attacks and weaknesses. Today keys may be distributed via the network itself, using a hierarchy of keys. The idea is that the master key, used to encrypt the message or session keys, is used so seldom that it will probably never be exposed. And once the master key is in place, secure communications among the holders of the master key can be ensured.

Various distribution and control schemes are used to distribute keys to those who will share the protected information. One of them works like this:

1. The security manager for the network delivers, by hand, a secret master encryption key to each person who will use the system. In some cases, this key is read into an electronic encryption system unit by means of light emissions from a key generator. This master key will authenticate these users each time information is to be transmitted.
2. When a message or file must be sent in protected mode, the network control center prepares a secret session key, which is encrypted using the master key. The session key can now be safely sent to the message addressee, without fear that an eavesdropper or interceptor will obtain it from the network. The

recipient can decipher the session key, using the previously delivered master key.

3. The message or file can now be encrypted using the session key, then sent to the addressee, who will decipher the message using the session key provided for this one message or set of messages. (A session can be any time set.)

It is important to recognize that the keys are critical and must be kept secret (if the data are to be effectively protected) and preserved (if the data are to be recovered).

Several clever methods have been developed to allow communication without hand-delivering a master key. In one case the sender provides the recipient with thousands of cryptograms, via the network; the recipient uses his or her computer to solve one cryptogram or puzzle, then returns the puzzle in plaintext, as a pointer to the part of the puzzle that will form the key. An eavesdropper would have to solve all the puzzles, which would be prohibitively time-consuming.

Many encryption systems can be implemented so as to provide automated key management based on time parameters or other controls. When initially installed, however, a network system usually requires the secure delivery of the initial authentication master key to each network node, usually by trusted courier.

Public Key System

The public key encryption method is based on the properties of very large prime numbers. Mathematicians have been unable to develop a means of finding the roots of a product of two large prime numbers. This fact allows encryption to be based on two keys, one public and one private. The public key is published in a directory; the private key is held secret by its owner.

Whitfield Diffie and Martin Hellman first suggested the concept of a public key system in 1976. They proposed using an encryption algorithm (EA) and a decryption algorithm (DA) so that deriving the DA would be impossible even if an expert cryptographer knew the EA. The algorithms that passed this test were developed by some researchers at MIT in 1978. The system works because of the difficulty involved in finding the factors of a product of two very large prime numbers.

To send a message, the sender looks up the recipient's public key in a published list and encrypts the message using that key. The message is secure because there is no way to decipher it without the private key, which is held only by the addressee. The public key system also allows a message to be "signed," that is, authenticated as to the sender. The authentication occurs when the sender encrypts the message by using both the recipient's public key and his or her own private key. The recipient applies his or her secret key in a first step. The recipient then proves the authenticity of the message by decrypting it again, using the sender's public key.

Technical details of the public key system may be found in a paper by Rivest, Shamir, and Adelman (1977), the developers of the concept. The public key system is now available commercially from RSA Data Security Inc. of Redwood City, California.

Encryption Applications in Networks

Generally, we can describe encryption applications in networks as being one of two types, message encryption or general encryption. Message encryption refers to the encrypting of certain messages or traffic on the network. General encryption refers to the use of encrypted data for general purposes, such as for security control.

Message Encryption

Certain messages or files may have a security flag set in the header, indicating that encryption is required; the sending network node or connected device then calls an encryption routine that encodes the message. Otherwise, messages may be received for entry to the network with physical or logical notations as to protection requirements. The sender may then process the message through an encryption software or hardware system. The message encryption application is an as-required process; that is, the service is always available.

Another message encryption application is link encryption. A company may decide that most high-value traffic flows over a few links in its network. The company installs encryption hardware at both ends of the links, and all traffic flowing over those links is encrypted, including ordinary traffic. The reasoning here is that the few high-value files or messages being sent over the open links of the network are less susceptible to eavesdropping; the cost of watching thousands of messages to find one valuable file is too great to make a penetrator's time worthwhile. But the links that frequently carry high-value messages are protected all the time. This minimizes encryption costs while protecting the majority of the company's high-value traffic.

Personal computer users can install encryption software packages on their microcomputers. When the user wishes to encrypt a file, either for transmission on a network or for disk file protection, he or she merely calls the encryption program, which then processes the data file into cyphertext. Many personal computer security packages include an encryption process as a standard feature. Personal computer users must be especially careful about handling the encryption keys. Using them is very different from using a password, which may be replaced if lost, or a damaged file, from which useful data may be recovered. Encrypted information is permanently encyphered (and unusable) unless the correct key is at hand.

End-to-end encryption means that a message or file is encrypted at its source and is decrypted only after it has reached its ultimate destination. When information must travel through a complex of links and nodes, or when it must go through several interconnected networks (for example, from a LAN via a wide area network to a second LAN), end-to-end encryption appears to be more secure than a link application. Obviously, if the message must be decrypted as it moves across each interlink switch, a risk is incurred at each such point.

There are arguments for and against both kinds of encryption:

For Link Encryption

- Subversion of one link by someone who develops a key does not destroy the security of other links.
- Full text, including headers and routing data, can be encrypted; traffic analysis from a tap of a link would be impossible.
- Other traffic on the link, all of it encrypted, would seem to be a good cover for the really valuable messages.
- Link encryption is less dependent on software, which could have faults, as it is usually implemented in hardware.

For End-to-End Encryption

- Information is always encrypted, which is especially important when data traverses public utility switches or circuits.
- Since a path may not be fixed, the message may be handled by a link in which the encryption service is inoperative or not provided.
- Key distribution is much simplified in that session keys must be sent only to the recipient.
- Misrouting should result in the wrong party receiving only cyphertext (that is, nonintelligible text).

General Applications of Encryption

A general application of encryption is for authentication in a local area or wide area network. A network control center or clearinghouse may be able to generate keys. Encryption services may be provided for certain links on the network or may be callable by users on a LAN.

We can use the XNS LAN as an example. Because the LAN is essentially an open system, access to system resources can be obtained by any user. This is a convenience for users, but it may represent a serious security vulnerability. We may wish to restrict users to certain resources or to restrict resources to certain users. In XNS the access control mechanisms and the authentication process provide controls. All users and servers must be able to trust the system to correctly identify users and servers, then authorize activities per network management's directions. Specially encrypted passwords and synchronized clocks are used to authenticate network users. Passwords are used to identify each user; when entered into a workstation on the XNS, the user password is immediately encrypted using the DES. The network thus ensures that a user password is never transmitted as clear text. This authentication process is a complex one that provides for very rigorous proof (see Figure 1.5).

Current research at Digital Equipment Corporation shows that effective encryption of information on Ethernet-based LANs will probably require two different encryption methods (Sebring 1987). This is so because of technical constraints on the various network layers in the ISO's architecture for LANs. One type of encryption is needed for local workstation to file server processes; the other is needed for internetworking applications. To date, LAN suppliers have not provided simple, integral encryption methods for all cases. Users who need comprehensive encryption services immediately are faced with adding on local service software and, probably, hardware for internet capability.

PART III

Achieving
Network Security

FIVE

Keys to Secure Network Operations

In contrast to the traditional data center/mainframe computer security situation, where regulations can be enforced through supervision and logical controls, a network of microcomputer workstations is a collection of hundreds and perhaps even thousands of individual users, invisible to management and perhaps unknown and unrecognized. Yet the protection of the critical information resource must rely on these people, spread across the company and maybe across the world, being willing and able to practice good security discipline when they use their workstations and the company's networks.

This is an age of skepticism. People want to know why before they agree to cooperate in any venture. This rule applies especially to security, as many protection measures are nuisances and seem to get in the way. Security regulations, or standards, must be based on well-conceived policies and must reflect the real working environment in the company. They must be seen as reasonable in light of the operational needs and security exposures of the business.

No matter what other measures are taken—direct management orders, advertising in company magazines, logical security systems, supervisory attention, and so on—all will be to little avail unless the employees perceive the regulations as being relevant and appropriate. In other words, the security standards must be of top quality.

CHARACTERISTICS OF EFFECTIVE
SECURITY STANDARDS

Good security standards have certain characteristics, no matter where they are to be used. They must be:

1. Complete. They must include all circumstances and situations normally encountered in the course of business operations.
2. Accessible. They must be delivered and presented conveniently for all employees, both as motivators and as detailed references.

3. Helpful. Standards must be perceived as contributing to the fulfillment of overall job responsibilities of the employees.
4. Consistent. Protection requirements must be consistent across the various kinds of company functions and among the types and forms of information.
5. Current. Good security standards reflect the current technology and practices of today's business operations.
6. Presented in different forms. They must be delivered in several forms so that a vital, relevant, and motivational message is continually provided.

Let's see how we can provide these characteristics in a program of security standards.

Standards Must Be Complete

The security standards must address all the situations and environments found in the company's operating activities. Consider a typical multinational manufacturing business. People will be using network-connected workstations on the factory floor, in offices at local sites and in company headquarters, in research laboratories, in engineering centers, in sales offices, in warehouses, and in many other locations. The security standards must provide answers to the question "What am I supposed to do to protect company information?"

That does not mean that we have to publish a separate standard for each work situation. But we do have to provide standards for those cases that have significantly different security requirements. One reason why we must do this is to make access to the security rules convenient to the appropriate people. We cannot expect every secretary to read about the things we might expect a research scientist to do, and vice versa.

We may envision a two-dimensional matrix as representing our requirements for completeness. On one plane we have the generic job types, which may include secretaries and office workers, research and engineering principals, managers, and so on. On the other plane we list the activities that must be addressed for each job type. These activities include creating files and documents, sending messages, forwarding messages, receiving messages, storing files and documents, and so forth. The items on the matrix will be slightly different for each business, but the matrix is important because it lets us see the security instructions that must be included in our standards to ensure that they are complete (see Figure 5.1).

Finally, complete standards provide a necessary supervisory tool. Supervisors can expect people to follow reasonable, published rules that are relevant to the employees' jobs.

Standards Must Be Accessible

This may seem to be a silly requirement, but in ten years of experience, it always surprises me to find that many employees say, "I knew there was something I

Job Types

Processes		Executive	Researcher	Engineer	Secretary	Accountant	Analyst
Messages	Encrypt high value						
Filing	Pass-word protects all						
Document Creation	N/A						
Marking High Value	Generate markings						
Using Distribution Lists							
CAD/CAM	N/A						

Figure 5.1   Matrix worksheet for developing standards.

should do, but I didn't know how to find out what I should do." This may be a weak excuse, but a good security program eliminates excuses by making the rules readily available everywhere company employees are at work. The delivery of security standards should be in the form and by the means suitable to the company's work practices. For example:

- Security standards can be made available in a public file on the network(s). In some companies, the number of employees having a desktop workstation or personal computer already approaches 75 percent. For these people, it may be easiest to read security standards directly from an on-line file. If the standards are organized by audience group (as are the standards shown in Chapter Six), this method of distribution is especially appropriate.
- Security standards can be published in a pocket-size booklet and distributed through general company mail (perhaps using the address list for the company newsletter or magazine) or by using booklet boxes at employee entrances. For some reason people like to pick up attractive booklets; perhaps they even read through them.
- Security standards can be distributed through group management; for example, to all scientists through the chief scientist. Using a management cascade

(top to bottom) for delivery gives any kind of directive an aura of authority. When one's boss hands out a directive, it is unlikely to be discarded peremptorily.

- Every security manager should have a company security handbook, and the network security standards should be included therein. A key to understanding is the availability of a live explanation of a requirement. The security coordinators and security managers must be prepared to answer questions or, in some difficult cases, to find the answers.

The concept of a security coordinator network is most helpful. The security coordinator, an employee with an extra assigned responsibility for security, provides an excellent distribution channel for security standards and their message. In some companies special distribution channels are set up to move materials to the local security coordinators who are closest to the action.

We must eliminate reasons why people do not know what is expected of them. Good standards are always accessible to those who want to find out.

Standards Must Be Helpful

Well-designed standards help people who want to practice security by defining the correct ways to protect information. Writing helpful standards is not an easy task, however. Helpful standards cannot be written at headquarters or by a staff member; rather, they are written by people with practical experience in the various business disciplines.

The security standards might be prepared by a committee representing the various operating groups, divisions, or sections of the business. The committee members bring their knowledge of the operating practices and business problems of each division or department. They can make sure that each standard fits within the operating environment of the particular organization. As a result of a committee approach, standards are a consensus, a compromise among varying positions. A standard which is 100 percent correct in the eyes of top management or senior staff may bring satisfaction to some, but compliance does not automatically follow.

Good standards represent the best that can be attained across the company. For example, some committee members may believe that passwords should be changed every thirty days, but if that requirement would be viewed as unreasonable by other groups, a compromise of every sixty days is much better than a rule that some groups will choose to disregard.

A helpful standard is one that is seen by most employees as a practical guide to securing information, given the work environment and the traditional operational practices of the company. As we will see below, security standards produced in different forms allow the contents to be paraphrased to provide really helpful job-related instructions.

Standards Must Be Consistent

Effective security standards are always consistent with other company policies and practices. This requires careful research. For example, at a large manufacturer, a policy requires that confidential documents may not be allowed to lie on a desk unattended for more than two hours. Beyond that time, the documents must be locked away. When network security standards were first developed, terminal devices connected to networks were required to have an automatic disconnect after a maximum time of thirty minutes. This was seen as an inconsistency by many who argued that a display was no different than a paper lying on a desk (although the display could not be carried off). Although in some cases the time to shutoff of a terminal should have been less, it was vitally important to have a consistency between the requirements for paper and displayed documents. After all, sensitive information can be picked up by access to either. The standard for displays was changed from thirty minutes to two hours.

Confusing instructions or rules that obviously are inconsistent negate the best efforts at motivation. Only consistent standards provide a rational, repeated message to employees.

Standards Must Be Current

Properly written policies should not require frequent revision; at best, policies should last up to ten years. If policies require frequent change, they are probably mixed up with procedures or standards. Standards, on the other hand, should be reviewed and changed regularly. A minimum cycle, based on typical technological development and application in business today, is about every three years. Examples of recent applications that have required standards modifications are the use of LANs, data downloading to personal computers, radio wave emanations from display tubes, and computer aided design (CAD) systems. New technologies and applications almost always are cause for a questioning review of security standards. Security vulnerabilities that do not fit existing published security standards are severe exposures.

Current security standards mean that employees will find answers to questions regarding up-to-date business practices, new technology, and innovative applications. When new network applications or technologies are introduced, a temporary or interim standard can be published in booklet form until a new set of official standards can be developed in the next review cycle.

Standards Must Be Presented in Different Forms

The security standards, per se, are published in some authoritative book, such as the company's security guide. Other copies may be placed in the information systems manual and in the security manager's handbook. But copies of the standards themselves may not be effective for the average employee for several reasons. The employee may not need to see all the contents of the standards and may not have a convenient way to maintain separate pieces of paper. Information outside formal binders or special electronic files tends to disappear after a while.

Security standards should be published as booklets, in a convenient size for a desk drawer or pocket. Paraphrased standards can be produced as special audience pieces—for example, as a folder or pamphlet titled "A Security Guide for Users of Office Systems." Or booklets or pamphlets can be produced relating to a specific piece of general use equipment—for example, "How to Use Facsimile Transmission Securely." These booklets could be delivered with the equipment when it is installed.

For a large company, a periodic newsletter summarizing new security developments, issues, problems, and solutions is a good way to stimulate awareness and remind people about security standards. The company newspaper or magazine could be used to publicize a contest or an employee awareness campaign. Posters, stickers, and convenience articles (paperclip holders, rulers, and so on) also are good ways to remind employees about the importance of protecting information.

Effective standards, and the more important messages therein, are always presented in several different forms, thus allowing employees to choose the form best suited to their job or situation and continually reminding them of their security responsibilities.

SPREADING THE WORD

The security coordinator network described earlier is a good medium for distributing standards materials. People respond to peer pressure more than to any other source. Security coordinators, being employees at the working level, are in an excellent position to distribute security materials, pamphlets, and posters and to explain to employees why their cooperation is important. Once information protection becomes an accepted practice for a majority of employees, peer pressure will do most of the work. At the Eastman Kodak Company, for example, years of practice have resulted in an environment in which all employees know that company information is not to be discussed outside the workplace.

Special arrangements, through the company mail room or facilities department, may facilitate putting up security posters on a regular basis. Some companies even have special frames mounted at strategic locations throughout offices and plants just for security posters.

SUMMARY

Getting all employees to follow security rules when connected to a network or when using information systems requires training and motivation. Supervision and security standards are essential. Security standards require a lot of thinking, working, and advertising to be effective. The set of qualities presented in this chapter defines effective security standards. A committee structure is best for developing and periodically renewing these standards. Good network security standards will help ensure that your security will be truly effective.

SIX

Security Standards for Modern Networks

Good security standards form the basis for securing business information processed or distributed on networks. Standards should be based on published company security policies (Herman, Haverty, and Dern 1986). The standards must provide all the guidance necessary for employees to act in a manner that will provide continuing protection to business information. To that end, standards should be published in several different forms (for example, booklets and posters).

While policy forms the bedrock for building a security program, standards ensure consistency of compliance with policy. Standards do this by defining the general protection measures required in all circumstances encountered in business operations. Should more detailed procedures be required, these can be published locally by the various divisions or offices.

In today's business environment, security standards should be written for the entire information network, not just for data centers or local processing situations. Effective network security standards address the total network environment and should establish security protection elements at the following four levels:

1. The wide area network level, using a central network management facility that can centrally handle encryption keys to protect data transmission sessions for authenticating users to one another and to network nodes and that can monitor network activity against established criteria.
2. The central computer level, usually by means of a security software package that uses individual user profiles to identify accessors and authorize actions.
3. The LAN level, using software facilities built into communications servers and clearinghouse servers.
4. The workstation level, usually by means of software packages run on individual personal computers or intelligent workstations.

Here we show a complete set of security standards for a large business operating a number of interconnected networks, including both wide area trunk lines and LANs. These standards are organized for convenience of reference by network and systems users, not for security technicians. Security measures must be provided in convenient form for business users to apply to protect all applications on the network.

NETWORK SECURITY STANDARDS*

THE GENERAL SECTION

(Author's note: This section explains those requirements that apply in every case. These are fairly broad, since we must assume that the overall security for a network of workstations and computers is equal to that of the weakest device or link.)

All employees have a responsibility for protecting company information. This requires:

- Making timely classification decisions.
- Using appropriate security measures and diligent care.

Quality business information has the characteristics of reliability (available when and where needed), integrity (complete, accurate, free from unauthorized change), and privacy (not exposed to unauthorized parties). Security is an essential element, along with good systems design, supervision, and training, in providing quality information business purposes.

Purpose

These standards implement company security policies. They deal with the protection of company information in electronic forms when processed or moved about on networks of computers, terminals, and special devices.

Responsibilities

Employees managing or using electronic information systems (including but not limited to word processors, workstations, intelligent copiers, computer terminals, network devices, network printers, and CAD/CAM/CAE systems) are responsible for understanding and compliance.

---

*Portions of the standards courtesy of Xerox Corporation.

For assistance, ask your unit security manager or local electronic security coordinator.

(Author's note: These standards start off by establishing that security is everybody's business, a necessary approach when dealing with today's vast networks.)

Exceptions

Where valid business reasons indicate alternative protection methods, the exception process (see below) applies.

Definitions

Access Management Controls: The process that applies procedural and logical *security elements* to ensure

- **Identification** of network and/or device users, through the presentation of a unique personal token—that is, something that the user has (plastic card), knows (password), or is (fingerprint, voice). Identification tokens are usually codes (passwords, ID numbers, account numbers, etc.) that are individually assigned but not necessarily secret.
- **Authentication** of claimed identity, through a secondary means of identification (one of the tokens described above) that is private to an individual and kept secret.
- **Authorization** to perform specified actions by match of an authenticated user against a predefined set of access privileges.
- **Monitoring of system activities** through regular observation of network and computer system activity logs and records, especially exceptional items that appear to be abnormal.

(Author's note: Access management controls are the basis for network security, since they allow us to fix responsibility to individual users.)

Clean Desk: The practice that requires all business information to be removed from view or otherwise protected when the workplace is unoccupied for periods of two hours or more. For systems users, this means taking action to place a terminal or microcomputer in an idle mode, returning magnetic media to secure storage locations, and otherwise ensuring that unauthorized parties cannot gain access to business information.

Downloading/Uploading: The retrieval of an entire file of data from a mainframe database / the reloading of a file to a central database; usually in relation to a network-connected microcomputer process.

Electronic Security Coordinator: An employee assigned an additional responsibility to serve as the department or office advisor on electronic security matters.

He or she ensures general awareness of and compliance with these standards by providing assistance to managers and employees as needed.

Electronic Security Levels: The classes or types of protective measures—that is, physical, procedural, and logical. Within each level are the electronic security elements (below).

Electronic Security Elements: The basic building blocks for constructing protective barriers such as

- **Physical elements:** door locks, guards, closed circuit television monitors, trespass alarms, entry control systems, shielding to minimize emanations, and so on.
- **Procedural elements:** records of employee authorizations to access information, password change histories, and computer use logs; actions to monitor records, inspect systems software changes, control documentation changes, and separate duties as appropriate.
- **Logical elements:** software and hardware functions that control network user activity and provide for identification, authentication, and authorization of users to access network resources or data base computers, process information, or encrypt high-value information.

Exception to Policy: An approval at a senior management level of a decision to use alternative protection measures or to accept unusual risks for business purposes.

Network System Administrator: The employee responsible for maintaining efficient service for users of a LAN; the system administrator is responsible for the security of the LAN components and for advising users on network security measures.

Prime User: The manager responsible for the information processed (the data owner) or the manager responsible for budgeting for or controlling the information system.

User: The end user or system user—that is, the employee using a system or device such as a terminal, minicomputer, microcomputer, word processor, electronic typewriter, Telecopier, personal workstation, CAD/CAM/CAE/device, and so on.

(Author's note: The definitions in this section are important if the company is to obtain the cooperation of all employees using network-connected devices. Understanding the terminology is a prerequisite to compliance.)

Implementing the Standards

Responsibilities

Employees (users) are responsible for protecting information in all forms. Employees may not use electronic information networks or systems for purposes other than those authorized by the responsible manager.

Electronic Security and Network System Administrators are responsible for assisting employees and managers in the fulfillment of electronic security responsibilities and will provide such advice and expertise as necessary. Problems or incidents must be promptly reported to the appropriate security manager.

Managers are responsible for controlling employee use of networks, information systems, and any connected devices. Effective controls include appropriate supervision, regular periodic security reviews, analysis of computing spending reports, and the application of a network access management control system.

NETWORK ACCESS MANAGEMENT CONTROL SYSTEMS

Computers and devices connected to networks (directly or via dial-up) or processing company classified information require the following controls:

1. A unique, personal identification token (for instance, an employee ID or account code) must be assigned to each user.
2. A unique, personal authentication token (such as a password, fingerprint, code generator, or combination thereof) must be used to validate the identity claimed. Passwords must be kept secret. To be effective, passwords should have at least six characters and must be changed at least every thirty days. Systems software or systems administration shall enforce such changes. Authentication tokens shall be handled and stored in the network and in individual computing systems in encrypted form and must never be displayed in cleartext.
3. The system authorization process controls user activity by referring to a list of objects (files, records, data types, hardware devices, and programs) allowed and by referring to a level of access (read/copy, update, create/delete, execute) as established by the prime user.
4. For classified information, individual need-to-know access privileges must be established, and the system must limit access and subsequent activity accordingly; for high-value information, the system also must provide user activity logs.
5. The system must suppress display of the authentication token and limit unsuccessful attempts to sign on to some reasonable number of tries (maximum of ten). The system logs any such unsuccessful attempts. The log should be monitored. Continuous unsuccessful attempts at sign-on should result in suspension of account privileges pending investigation.
6. Administrative controls must ensure that access authorizations are canceled or changed upon employee job change (which modify need-to-know status), transfer, or termination. Such control usually involves cancellation of user

accounts. This should be done through a formal mechanism, preferably tied to personnel employee processing procedures.

7. Devices left unattended in active mode must be automatically shut off, returned to idle mode, or otherwise protected consistent with the clean desk policy.

8. Access to information processing resources from dial-up origins must be controlled through programmed modems, callback systems, or other port control methods to meet the access management control criteria.

9. A network control center shall monitor wide area network activity. Link encryption services shall be made available when traffic warrants.

(Author's note: In a number of cases above, one sees that security measures are designed to minimize business costs and to allow judgment on the part of managers.)

INFORMATION PROTECTION REGULATIONS

Company information classifications are assigned by the prime user or by the user in situations where personal computing (including word processing) may generate new information. The information classifications and protection requirements are explained in detail in company information management standards. Briefly, these requirements are as follows:

*   **High Value** is the highest classification. This is information that, if disclosed, could cause serious damage to the operation of the company. Encryption of such information is required when transmitted over telecommunications circuits and when stored on nonremovable magnetic media (removable media must be stored in a bar-lock cabinet or safe). All security elements levels must be applied. Access is allowed only to specifically identified individuals.
*   **Private Data** are pieces of information that, if disclosed, could have a substantially detrimental effect on the company.
*   **Personal Data** are pieces of information that, if disclosed, might be embarrassing or detrimental to an individual or the company. For either private or personal data, appropriate security elements must be applied to prevent unauthorized disclosure, modification, or destruction. Access is allowed only to those employees who have a need to know.

All other company information is for internal use only unless publicly announced or published.

The transfer of technical or personal data to persons or organizations outside the originating country may be controlled by government regulations and by company contractual obligations. Criminal penalties often apply to violations.

For details, see the appropriate data protection officer, export/import coordinator, or legal counsel.

General Marking and Handling Requirements

Company classified information must be protected from casual observation at all times. Such classified information in visual display or document forms must be clearly marked with the appropriate symbol or computer-generated equivalent, of sufficient size to be obvious. Documents must be protected at all times in process, storage, and delivery.

When unattended network output devices (such as facsimile machines or network printers) are used, special arrangements must be made to ensure that company classified information is fully protected from loss, copying, or unauthorized observation.

NONCOMPANY AND OUTSIDE SERVICES AND CONNECTIONS

Objective

To ensure consistent protection of information when processed in computers operated by other than the company; when noncompany originated application software and/or services are used; and when company computers or networks are directly connected with such devices operated or controlled by others.

(Author's note: The control of information when company networks are interconnected with outside trunk networks operated by public utilities, or with networks of other companies, suppliers, consultants, or legal counsel, is critical.)

Scope

All employees using outside computing or telecommunications services or approving external interconnections.

Definitions

Outside Services: Any services involving electronic information processing and/or transfers provided by noncompany parties.
External Interconnections: Any direct telecommunications connections established between company computer/network resources and noncompany parties/networks/computing sources. This definition does not include the use of

basic telephone or telecommunications service utilities (such as AT&T, British Telecom, or TYMNET) for connections between company-operated computers or devices or as part of a company wide area network or internet. It also does not include the use of general public services such as Dun & Bradstreet, travel reservation systems, or others that involve public services or one-way retrieval of information.

Requirements

Managers will take necessary actions to ensure continuing protection as follows:

1. High-value information may not be processed by outside services or transmitted via company internal networks, by external interconnections, including ARPANET and Telex, or by other general communications utilities (such as AT&T, British Telecom, and the PTTs) unless encrypted.
2. Applications software developed by outside parties may not be used to process high-value information unless approved on an exception basis. A list of such software, approved per the exception process, may be established by organizations processing such information regularly. Qualifying applications software must meet all the other security requirements of these standards.
3. Private data and personal data may not be processed by outside services unless approved on an exception basis. Prudent care must be used when sending information in these classifications by Telex or other general communications utilities that are not secure against casual observation.
4. Local area network external interconnections are not permitted except for mail service via mail gateways implemented through approved products only. Any other connection to company networks requires an exception approval.
5. Where dial-up connections to computing resources involve access to classified information, special controls must be applied. These may include (1) a software control package such as ACF2, RACF, or similar; (b) use of a port protection device (callback); (c) encryption; (d) a manual procedure to identify callers; (e) a combination of these elements appropriate to the company classification assigned to the information handled.
6. Connections with persons or systems in countries outside the originating country require special care to ensure compliance with national export control regulations, data transfer laws, and contractual obligations. (For further information, see your export control coordinator, data security officer, or legal counsel.)
7. Systems processing personal information must comply with national or other applicable privacy laws in all places to or from which data are transmitted.

(Author's note: Many countries now have privacy laws; extreme care must be taken when using networks crossing national boundaries.)

INFORMATION PROCESSING
AND TELECOMMUNICATIONS

Objective

To ensure that data processing centers and telecommunications operations organizations have security sufficient to ensure consistent protection of company information.

Requirements

Responsibilities. Managers of information processing and telecommunications service organizations are responsible for the protection of information entrusted to their care for processing and/or transmission, in accordance with company classifications and the organization's implemented electronic security elements.

General. Information processing and telecommunications service organizations shall normally provide security at the level required for company private data. To that end, a set of security element offerings shall be made available, including a wide area network control system and an Access Management Control software package; prime users and users may select appropriate protection means from this set of security services. The security protections will be maintained consistently throughout networks and distributed systems, and in accordance with applicable privacy legislation.

Environmental. Positive physical security elements for access control will be established, both for entry to the general facility and for entry to more restrictive areas (such as operations or the media library).

Input/Output. Company information must be protected at all times whether in electronic or printed form. Outputs must be properly marked or stamped and delivered in a controlled manner.

Operational. Information processing and telecommunications service organizations must exercise positive control over operating system and hardware maintenance activities, processor loading and systems clock setting, and changes to operating documentation. An audit trail of all systems activities must be maintained and reviewed.

Magnetic Media. Information processing and telecommunications service organizations must provide for secure storage, handling, and shipping of tapes, disks, cartridges, or other media. Release of any media must be strictly controlled based on company information security practices and need-to-know requirements for the various classifications (see General section). Shipments of media must be by courier, receipted delivery, or other secure means. Media must be securely packed with classification labels on the internal reel or disk and addressee only on the outside package. Periodic inventories of media are required to maintain effective control.

DISTRIBUTED COMPUTING, INCLUDING
PERSONAL, OFFICE, RESEARCH, AND SCIENTIFIC

(Note: This part of the standards is extremely important, since the crux of our concern about networks has to do with individual employee access to and use of network facilities.)

Objective

To maintain consistent protection for company information in all forms and at all stages of processing or handling.

Requirements

Responsibilities

Employees using personal workstations of all types, including microcomputers, terminals, facsimile devices, communicating copiers, network-connected printers, communicating typewriters, and similar devices, are responsible for the protection of company information processed. Employees also must

1. Maintain a secure, controlled workplace per the clean desk policy.
2. Protect company classified information on the network.
   a. High-value information must be encrypted for transmission on any network.
   b. Never send company classified information to an uncontrolled distribution list (DL), which may contain unknown names. Controlled DLs with <Friends:Nil> specified may be used with care. It is the responsibility of the message sender to determine that the DL will deliver the information only to those employees authorized to have it and that the DL owner is reliable.
   c. When classified information is involved, always use the strong authentication password (when such option is available).
   d. A message containing company classified information must have the reply-to field filled in to ensure that replies are not delivered to unauthorized persons.
   e. Ensure security of classified documents produced on network print servers by picking up documents promptly or by making other arrangements to ensure information privacy.
   f. Information that is critical to operations should be stored in two places—

for example, desktop and floppy, desktop and file drawer (file service), file drawer and floppy.

3. Use proper password discipline.
   a. Passwords must be kept secret.
   b. To be effective, passwords should have at least six characters and must not be easily guessed.
   c. Passwords must be changed at least every thirty days.

4. Back up files as appropriate to ensure continued business operation.

5. Report security problems to supervisor, systems administrator, or local network service center manager.

6. Shield company classified information from casual view while on VDT screen or desk; place electronic systems in idle mode when away from the workplace for more than two hours or less as locally appropriate.

7. Properly protect, mark, and store company classified outputs and magnetic media (tapes and disks).

8. Never use software developed outside the company for processing company classified information unless such software has been certified as acceptable by the unit information systems manager.

9. Never upload locally processed information to central database files unless the upload is a routine processing task controlled by the receiving data center and established as part of a regularly scheduled data system.

(Author's note: The above instructions for the individual employee are in sufficient detail to allow for extraction and republication as a pamphlet or folder.)

Electronic Security Coordinators ensure general awareness of and compliance with these standards, and provide advice and assistance to network users as needed.

Systems Administrators for LANs must

1. Provide security instructions to network users, working closely with the organizational security coordinator in this effort.

2. Maintain privacy of passwords and files entrusted to their care.

3. Ensure proper physical security protection for Internet file servers and communication servers.

4. Work with network users to ensure proper document handling in cases where shared print facilities produce Xerox classified information.

5. Provide backup files for information on file servers in line with established schedules and contingency plans.

6. Report network security problems or incidents to supervisor, local security manager, and network management.

Managers are responsible for establishing effective controls over company information by

1. Training employees in information protection procedure. Those employees

with operational/technical duties (such as systems administrators and software/hardware maintenance specialists) must be made aware of their special security responsibilities.

2. Controlling proper authorization to use electronic information processing/communicating equipment and by monitoring proper Access Management Control discipline, including ensuring that access privileges are properly canceled upon employee job change or separation.

3. Providing suitable physical and logical security elements for employee workplaces, with special attention to general purpose computers or other information processors that may be situated in offices, plants, or other areas not designated as data centers.

4. Planning for contingency actions for recovery in event of disaster.

5. Establishing clear responsibility for systems-related actions, including Access Management Control, and providing for separation of duties where sensitive responsibilities are to be met (such as in systems software maintenance).

6. Assigning the electronic security coordinator responsibilities as appropriate; assigning security responsibilities to systems administrators as appropriate.

7. Providing suitable shielding to prevent emanations when high-value information is processed in a location subject to radio interceptions.

EXCEPTIONS TO POLICY

Objective

To establish a procedure for management approval of decisions not to follow these standards. An exception to policy is an approval at a senior management level of a decision to use alternative protection measures or to accept unusual risks justified by business requirements.

Requirements

Responsibilities

Managers at all levels are responsible for ensuring continuing protection for information as specified in these standards. When business requirements so dictate, managers must obtain exception approval to use alternative protection methods or to accept unusual risks.

(Author's note: Since all business amounts to the taking of risks, it is reasonable to provide for controlled risk taking in the processing of information. This section provides for such decisions at the appropriate management level.)

Procedure

Exception to policy approvals must be obtained when:

1. Business requirements justify exceptions to these standards.

2. Business requirements make a limited acceptance of risk appropriate.
3. Unusual or severe risk is evident in a business proposal.
4. Supplier premises are to be used for processing company classified information.
5. Application-specific software developed outside the company is to be used for processing high-value information.
6. Network external interconnections, except for mail service via mail gateways, are implemented through approved products only. Any other connection requires an exception approval.
7. External interconnections are to be established between company computers/ devices/telecom networks and noncompany computers/devices/telecom networks.

Exception approval requests are to be processed as follows:

- *For high-value information:* A written risk analysis must be provided, to include the operating environment, a list of vulnerabilities and risks with probabilities assigned, potential results should an attack be successful, costs to the company of such a successful attack, and a comparison of the cost of the alternative with the application of protection required per this standard. The exception request must be concurred in by the manager of corporate security and approved in writing by a unit president, managing director, or equivalent.
- *For private or personal information:* A written risk analysis must be provided. The exception request must be approved in writing by a unit director or equivalent.
- *For all other information:* Exception request must be approved in writing by a unit vice president or equivalent.

SEVEN

Handling the Personal Computer Risk

The personal computer (PC) is probably the most significant technical advance of history, in terms of its potential effects on business. Although the time-sharing systems of a decade past allowed individuals to use a "slice" of the power of a large mainframe computer at a distant data center, the user was confined to the limited data entry and retrieval process imposed by a nonintelligent terminal. Now the PC, or more correctly the many forms of the microcomputer, allows the downloading (the retrieval of entire files from the central mainframe computer) of data, local processing using self-developed or purchased software, local data storage, and uploading of data items or files to the central processor. In addition, the modern telecommunications infrastructure and services array allows the PC user to perform prodigious feats of information transfer, across the office or across the world. All this means that information security must be rethought and carefully planned when and where personal computers are in use.

AN EXAMPLE

Personal computer user A subscribed to a public network service that included a feature called Chat. This allowed a signed-on service user to scan the network and exchange keyed-in messages with any other user also on the Chat board. During such an exchange of messages with unknown person B, user A sent a Control-C, or null command. B thought he had been disconnected and immediately signed on again, thus sending his account number and password to A. Thereafter, user A was able to use the system free—at B's expense, of course.

WHAT IS A PERSONAL COMPUTER?

Terminology in computing has always been confusing. The definition of a mainframe computer versus a minicomputer has always been in the eyes of the beholder. The microcomputer is usually referred to as a personal computer, but it has many forms. For our purposes here, we will use the term *personal computer,* or PC, to encompass all those intelligent devices that deliver computing power to the end user. These devices include, among others:

- Personal computers.
- Professional workstations (usually found in engineering, publishing, legal, and other detailed, specialized applications).
- Word processors.

Hardware

The PC always includes a processor, some memory for temporary data storage during processing, some form of permanent data storage (usually a disk), and a display (usually a video display tube but possibly a typewriter). The PC also may have a printer (local or shared), high-capacity disk storage, floppy disk drives, a plotter, a high-resolution windowed display, and/or a color display.

Software

The PC will always have an operating system, which consists of those programs provided by the computer manufacturer or by a software developer and which provides the instructions to the computer hardware for the processing of data. The PC also may use special software for driving attached devices. The PC's work is done through various applications programs, or software packages as they are called. These may include word processing packages, general purpose office systems providing windowing and icon displays, spreadsheet and analysis packages, graphics software, communications software, and an almost unlimited variety of packaged combinations of these and other features.

THE POWER OF THE PERSONAL COMPUTER

As a result of the impressive array of hardware and software facilities available, the PC user can do just about anything the data center manager could do ten years ago. The only difference may be in the size of files that can be processed; most PCs are not yet ready to do data base processing. The PC also has all the security vulnerabilities of a data center, except that those vulnerabilities are more severe because of the lack of formal control and procedural structure in any activity totally controlled by an individual. The PC user may be able to:

1. Retrieve data or entire files from a central computer or from connected data storage on a LAN's file servers. In effect, the PC can be used like a remote batch terminal.
2. Process that data using company-provided software, purchased software, self-developed software, or free software copied from a hacker's network. Software not produced and tested within company quality-assurance guidelines must be considered suspect at best.
3. Deliver the processed results to the central data base, a LAN file server, a printer, a plotter, or via a network to any place on earth. Whether or not the output file then becomes a matter of record, accepted by some or all as fact, remains a concern.
4. Combine the results of processing with other files locally held, at distant file servers on LANs, or on data base files in central computers. Data with hidden errors become more difficult to identify as they are mixed with other "good" (officially sanctioned) information.
5. Access innumerable files that are open to general network users or for which the user may have authority, and browse through those files, retrieve information, and assemble collections of data. Unless file access controls are widely used and effective, curious persons can stumble across sensitive, perhaps potentially dangerous, information combinations.
6. Even when not authorized access to files, the PC user may be able to run programs locally to develop access passwords and thus penetrate controlled files or processes. The PC user may be able to perform tricky manipulations of security controls or spoof authorized users to obtain access rights belonging to other users.
7. Perform all the processes listed in various locations—some private, some public—including working at home (with dial-in network connections) and while traveling (in hotels with dial-in network connections and on airplanes or in airport lounges). The potential for dial-in is a most serious threat to information privacy.

Consider each of these instances (not an exhaustive list) and figure out several ways in each case in which the company's requirement for quality information could be violated.

THREATS TO INFORMATION

We can suggest a number of major vulnerabilities of information when communicated or processed on network-connected PCs. *Physical threats* include theft of data on floppy disks or through the taking of a complete PC system; casual observation of sensitive information on a PC display; theft of printed output documents; and improper use of a keyboard or other entry device to penetrate security controls (allowing access to the single PC, its files, or the entire network) or cause information damage, loss, or exposure when a PC has been carelessly left in an active or connected state.

Logical threats include subversion of the operating system or its controls through improper (unauthorized) use of keyboard entry; subversion of PC controls through remote entry or spoofing via network connections; placing of Trojan horse or time-bomb software through the offer of free or for sale programs; loss of data privacy through unauthorized intentional or casual browsing in data files that may be on local PC data stores on hard disk or on LAN file servers. Recently, a research scientist has developed a "virus program," which finds its way from one network-connected processor to another and can eventually destroy files or take control of operating systems (Cohen 1985). The virus program has been demonstrated before various expert groups (U.S. Bureau of Standards/ Department of Defense Computer Security Conference, 1984).

Procedural threats include data exposure caused by the failure of a user to recognize the value of locally created information and hence neglecting to set company classification and to provide protection; penetration of controlled files or work spaces due to user-set weak passwords that may be easily guessed or continued use of old passwords that have been exposed; loss or exposure of private information because shared printers are not properly protected or because PC users fail to pick up or protect output documents; failure to install and use PC security software that allows for the protection of files through passwords or other means and for the protection of high-value files and communications through encryption; failure to plan for contingencies such as fire, theft, or loss of data through file system technical faults (crashes).

A new level of risk is created when employees take PCs home and do work there, perhaps via network connections with a central office or data base computer. The business is almost completely reliant on the employee's willingness to follow proper procedure in this case. What is to stop him or her from providing passwords to family members or from allowing disks with company data from being used for other purposes? Only motivation.

PROTECTING THE NETWORK-CONNECTED PERSONAL COMPUTER

Major data centers today are fairly well secured, almost without exception. They are surrounded by multiple levels of security, both physical and logical. A staff of technical security specialists and a force of guards make certain that protection is provided to meet company information security requirements.

The PC, on the other hand, is usually found in the typical office environment. While access to many business offices may be controlled through the use of identification cards or doors with digital combination locks, for all practical purposes most offices are semipublic. Yet an office complex of PCs connected to a LAN, with its attendant file servers, communications servers, and printers, is likely more powerful than the average data center.

There is probably no technical security staff, no central well-maintained security software system containing the authorized user profiles, and no restricted areas where only authorized personnel are allowed. Rather, the whole security responsibility rests with the collective individual user group. These people are the data center managers and the security managers, individually and collectively. The weak link theory definitely applies here.

Effective security for the network-connected PC requires that we (1) specify what we want people to do and (2) get them to want to do it. This motivation was covered earlier; here, we will consider the unique PC security requirements.

PLANNING FOR SECURE USE
OF PERSONAL COMPUTERS

We must assume that a business has considered, and made decisions about, the management of its information resource. These decisions on information structure, valuation, and protection are the bases on which an effective PC security program is built. The company should have decided on strategic purposes, applications, and controls for the network of interconnected PCs and for stand-alone PCs.

As applications move from the mainframe computers to PCs, and as innovative new applications are developed for networks of PCs, management must have in place a process for ensuring continuing information quality. That includes prudent measures for protecting information. These measures are to be implemented through a framework of directives, as described in Chapter Two.

Company Directives on Personal Computer Use

Every business should have established directives that spell out the business controls established for the use of PCs. Management planning, the prerequisite to directives, must include the following:

1.   A risk analysis to determine the particular vulnerabilities of the company when a network-connected PC is in use, at work or at home. From this analysis we discover the basic policy requirements—that is, what we must insist the employee do. The information vulnerabilities may be different for each application. One of the problems is that the company may not even know who is using PCs, let alone what they are doing with them. The policy and standards covering the use of PCs must then provide some control mechanism ensuring that the company will know whenever its information is being processed on a PC.

2.   A procedure on how PCs are to be obtained, used, and controlled. A PC must not be thought of as merely another piece of office equipment for several reasons, including compatibility with other equipment, effective use of software investments, and information control. Since a PC is so cheap (probably less than

$500 in the near future), employees can buy a PC casually, and managers can procure them using money designated for office supplies. The company needs strict rules about how any computing equipment is to be purchased; even better, the company should specify which PCs can be used, which operating systems are to be used, and some means of limiting application.

3.   A formal acceptance of responsibility by employees should they want to use a PC or other terminal device off the premises. The contract should establish in writing that the employee understands his or her responsibility for protecting company information processed and that the employee promises to follow company security practices. Businesses no longer may assume that "employment at will" is the rule; court decisions have established that the discharge of any employee must be for substantial and documented reason. Getting the employee to sign an agreement about PC use is good management.

4.   Controls to limit casual access to networks and mainframe computers. Of course, the company cannot control what employees do on their own time, but it can control access to computer ports, and this is the control point for PC connections to data base computers or networks. One method is to use one of the many port control systems now available. Some require the user to have a physical key that generates a code in the process of authentication. Such a system ensures that the user is precisely identified regardless of the equipment used or the location from which an access is attempted.

5.   A published policy on the use of software from sources outside the company. This is essential to ensure that control is maintained, especially where devices are connected with networks. The so-called hackers' bulletin board systems offer software for free or on an honor system, in which a user is asked to send payment. Use of such programs is very risky; the company should clearly establish, in writing, with each employee a responsibility for avoiding any software not officially approved.

Personal computer software not only represents an expensive asset, but it also may be a liability for the company should employees fail to abide by the contract obligations incurred when software packages are purchased for use. All PC software—for operating systems, utility programs (packages such as spreadsheet software), and applications programs (such as locally written budget analysis systems)—must be protected. The vulnerabilities of PC software include:

• Illegal copying or use of copyrighted software purchased under a contract license.
• Surreptitious modification of operating system, security control, or applications software on a disk, for fraud or other illicit purposes.
• Loss of software should the disk containing the programs be carelessly written over or erased, or should the disk be stolen.

Software must be protected in the same way as valuable data. Disks should always be clearly marked, including the classification marking if appropriate.

They should be stored in an organized manner so that a missing disk will be noticed. Locking cabinets or desk drawers should be provided to secure the disks when they are not in use.

In the booklet "Good Security Practices for Control of Off-Site Terminal and Software Usage" (IBM 1984), IBM suggests a number of excellent control requirements, including the following:

1.　Only those personal computers and software packages approved by the company may be used for company business. This is consistent with prudent information security rules on how company classified documents may be obtained and how they are to be protected if carried off the premises. Limiting the software to that approved by the company is essential to ensuring information integrity. Restricting the types of computers to be used contributes to the value of the company's PC software library and simplifies connectivity.

2.　The company's PC may be used only for company business. If the employee owns the PC, a policy should be set on whether it may be used for business and, if so, how information is to be controlled. A PC shared by the employee and family members is not a good idea.

3.　Company classified information may never be retrieved or entered from an off-site location. This rule reflects the fact that effective controls over information retrieval are difficult to establish once the terminal user is authenticated. To the computer, the path a message or file may take to an authenticated user is irrelevant; but from a security viewpoint, it is very important.

4.　Company classified information is never to be processed on a PC when outsiders are in the area. This seems to be a more general rule that would apply even when work is done inside the company. The need-to-know rule applies in every case.

5.　Each employee is personally responsible for protecting company classified information and for properly using company specified security measures. Individual understanding and motivation to use good security practices is a prime requirement when networks are in use. The implication here is that the employee has been provided security instructions.

6.　Each user must have a unique identifier and authenticator before signing on to the network. Authorities must never be shared; passwords or other tokens must be protected by the individual user.

7.　Passwords will be kept secret and changed periodically according to company standards. Companies that care about their information resource regard the privacy and protection of passwords or other authentication tokens to be a matter of trust. Violation is regarded as a most serious matter, often resulting in discharge.

8.　Network-connected PCs must be disconnected from the network or placed in an inactive state if the device is to be left unattended. The network itself can have a time-out device when no activity is evident.

9.　Periodically, management must review the justification for each employee's having a PC. The ownership and use of PCs at work should be a regular item in company audits. Periodic surveys against dial-in access logs might be a good way to check for off-premises use of PCs (Manganelli 1986).

Practical Security Measures for Personal Computers

We will break down the security measures required into the security element levels, as described earlier. These are physical, logical, and procedural security measures.

Physical Measures

Areas where PCs are used should be secured according to the company classification of the information processed. Except for high-value information, which may require special efforts, the PC usually is provided average office security.

Equipment should be provided with security fasteners to fix the units to the desk or floor, unless the area is considered secure when the building is not occupied. Secure storage must be provided for tapes and disks. This storage should have the same security protection level as that required for documents with the same company classification. In most cases, high-value information must be stored in a safe or bar-lock cabinet. Software is expensive and deserves to be stored in the same manner as valuable data.

Tapes and disks that have been used for sensitive information should never be returned to the manufacturer or sold as scrap. No matter what actions are taken to erase information on disks, technically clever ways can be found to retrieve it. Most erase commands merely blank out the file headers and reference table entries, but the data remain on the disk.

In certain circumstances, hardware locks (to disable the unit power supply, for example) may be appropriate. The advantage of considering the various levels of security elements is that one can often develop a simple, economical security solution. A simple lock on a PC or disk drive power supply may be such an answer, especially in secured business offices.

Logical Measures

Most PC operating systems (such as MS-DOS) have been developed with user convenience, not information security, in mind. Most PCs (except for very recent, more powerful models) do not have a system architecture that can effectively accommodate security mechanisms. One can say that most PC controls simply cannot be trusted to control system resources or data. For example, a PC disk operating system may provide file status designators of "read only" or "hidden." These flags provide some discretionary control, but the operating system flags that control these states are easily manipulated by anyone with a little technical cleverness. Files on "as delivered" PCs must be assumed to be available to anyone with physical access to the machine.

For an access control to be effective, a means must be provided to authenticate an individual user, thus differentiating one user from another. Of course, in a case where only one person uses a PC and physically controls access to it, this is a moot point. Every PC processing company classified information should be provided with a security control software package or with a combination software/hardware security package. These allow password controls to be set using software constructs or may use hand-held authentication devices that generate a signal via the PC's display screen in conjunction with added circuit boards.

These software packages come in a wide range of power and applications. Various privilege levels can be established and may be controlled by a PC administrator who has general access and administrative rights. Directories of sensitive files may be hidden so that a casual user will not see the file names. File encryption services may be offered as an option. Table 7.1 compares some popular PC operating systems and services.

Network-connected PCs must use the facilities of a central security program for authentication when the initial network connection is made (for connection with mainframes, ACF2, RACF, Top Secret, and so forth; for PCs connected with LANs, a security function in the clearinghouse). In addition to authenticating valid users, the security package also may be used to restrict user actions to those authorized by data owners. Several PC security control packages now offer optional features that allow an interface with mainframe security systems such as ACF2 and Top Secret.

An encryption system, preferably one that allows message authentication, is important when a PC will be used to communicate management strategy or to process high-value business data. Encryption is the strongest protection known, but it requires strict management of the encryption keys. If the keys are lost, the data also are lost.

Procedural Measures

All PC users or owners must be identified for management control purposes. Users should sign a receipt for equipment and software and a statement of responsibility. The serial number and location of each PC should be recorded and periodically verified.

Network and central computer security controls must be kept up-to-date with current employee job assignments. A process must be in place to ensure that authorizations are changed or canceled when employees leave the company or are transferred to other jobs.

Contingency plans should be drawn up, and carefully tested, for recovery of necessary business information should a fire or other disaster destroy personal computing resources. Individual users should be required to keep backup data disks, procedures, programs, and so forth to ensure recoverability.

Locally developed software (for example, applications programs developed by an individual for his or her own use in meeting a business responsibility) should be subjected to a quality test before being allowed to be put into use. These local software programs usually have not had the benefit of the formal

Table 7.1   Comparison of Personal Computer Operating Systems and Services

Operating System	Strengths	Weaknesses	Comment
CP/M 8-bit	Large software base CP/M plus has tree-structured directories and better help facilities	Poor messages No access control	Home user oriented
CP/M 16-bit Concurrent 3.1	Multitasking (four tasks); multi and single user Record and file locking Access controls available Ability to submit jobs	Needs powerful hardware Poor user interface	Can also run PC DOS
MS/DOS	Large software base Tree-structured directories Reasonable error messages Multiuser version— XENIX (based on UNIX) Ability to submit jobs User friendly	No access control but can be plugged in	Contender for future standard in education Known as PC DOS on IBM hardware
PICK	User friendly Multiuser Multitasking Protection of files Access controls File and record locking Includes relational database, word processing, data editor, and retrieval language Fast Virtual memory management Procedural job control language Spooling device	Needs powerful processor Only available on a few micros (68000-based machines)	Originally a minicomputer operating system An option for universal systems across mainframe/mini/micro

Table 7.1   *(continued)*

Operating System	Strengths	Weaknesses	Comment

UNIX	Multiuser
	Multitasking
	Very portable;
	  mainframe/mini/
	  micro
	Protection of files
	Access controls
	Supports relational
	  data bases
		Shell is not very user
		  friendly
		Needs large amounts
		  of disk space (1
		  MB RAM)
		Lack of business
		  software
		No record locking
			XENIX is a version
			  for the micro
			Started life as a
			  minicomputer
			  operating system

Reprinted by permission of The National Computing Centre, Ltd., from "Security in Office Systems."

quality assurance procedures established in professional programming and systems development groups. The code may contain serious errors, mistakenly or intentionally. Before management accepts the output data and relies on them, some objective review and testing of the software should be done, perhaps by company auditors.

Every PC user should have been provided with security responsibilities instruction, either through direct training or by means of a booklet or pamphlet.

SUMMARY

The PC and other microcomputer devices provide a tremendous boost to information handling and communication in business. But the devices, especially when connected to networks, constitute severe information security threats. Careful attention by management is needed to set strategies for PC use, establish security requirements and controls, and motivate employees to do what is necessary.

References

Blank, Mark M. 1986. "Microcomputing Comes of Age." *Journal of Systems Management,* June, pp. 32–33.

Cohen, Fred. 1985. *Computer Viruses.* Privately published.

Cotnoir, Marc. 1986. *Securing Local Area Networks.* Delran, NJ: Datapro Research Corporation, IS35 101.

Curtice, Robert M. 1986. "Getting the Data Base Right." *Datamation,* October 1, p. 99.

Davidson, John M., and Don Huntington. 1985. "LANS: On Their Way to Systems." *Telecommunications,* September, p. 53.

Diebold, John. 1979. "IRM: New Directions in Management." *Infosystems,* October, p. 41.

Ellison, J.R., and J.A.T. Pritchard. 1986. *Security in Office Systems,* Manchester, U.K.: The National Computing Centre, Ltd., pp. 16–24.

Feinstein, Hal. 1986. *Network Security.* American Society for Industrial Security, Annual Seminar, September.

Fidlow, Daniel. 1985. "Data Communications Security: A Comprehensive Approach." In *Interface '85,* New York: McGraw-Hill, pp. 100–112.

Herman, James, Jack Haverty, and Daniel Dern. 1986. "Wide Area Networks." *Telecommunications,* September, p. 103.

Hoffman, Lance J. 1977. *Modern Methods for Computer Security and Privacy.* Englewood Cliffs, NJ: Prentice-Hall, p. 10.

IBM Corporation. 1984. *Good Security Practices for Control of Off-Site Terminal and Software Usage,* December, G320–9295–0, p. 3.

Kang, Young Moo, et al. 1986. "Comments on Grosch's Law Revisited: CPU Power and the Cost of Computation." *Communications of ACM,* August, p. 779.

Kirkley, John L. 1986. "Viewpoint." *Computerworld,* August 25, p. 17.

Krauss, Leonard I., and Aileen MacGahan. 1979. *Computer Fraud and Countermeasures.* Englewood Cliffs, NJ: Prentice-Hall, p. 405.

"LANS—Growing, Growing, and Gone." 1986. *Computer Decisions,* Special Issue, October 28, p. 16.

"Making Better Use of Your Data." 1986. *EDP Analyzer,* August, pp. 4–5.

Manganelli, Raymond L. 1986. "In Rating MIS, Size Is Not the Real Issue." *Information Week,* October 6, p. 80.

Murray, William H. 1984. "Security Considerations for Personal Computers." *IBM Systems Journal* vol. 23, no. 3.

Naisbitt, John. 1982. *Megatrends.* New York: Warner Books.

Needham, Roger M., and Michael D. Schroeder. 1978. *Using Encryption for Authentica-*

tion in Large Networks of Computers. Palo Alto, CA: Xerox Palo Alto Research Center.

Quarterman, John S., and Josiah C. Hoskins. 1986. "Notable Computer Networks." *Communications of ACM,* October, pp. 932–971.

Rivest, R., A. Shamir, and L. Adelman. 1977. *A Method for Obtaining Digital Signatures and Public Key Cryptosystems.* Cambridge, MA: MIT Press, LCS/TM82.

Rutledge, Linda S., and Lance J. Hoffman. 1986. "A Survey of Issues in Computer Network Security." *Computers & Security* 5 (December), p. 296.

Schmucker, Kurt. 1983. *Fuzzy Sets, Natural Language Computation, and Risk Analysis.* Rockville, MD: Computer Science Press.

Schweitzer, James A. 1983. *Protecting Information in the Electronic Workplace.* Reston, VA: Reston Publishing Co., p. 87.

Schweitzer, James A. 1986. *Computer Crime and Business Information.* New York: Elsevier Science Publishers, p. 31.

Sebring, Jeff. 1987. *DEC Security Research.* Xerox Electronic Security Workshop, March.

Strassman, Paul A. 1985. *Information Payoff.* New York: The Free Press, pp. 88, 225.

Tanenbaum, Andrew S. 1981. *Computer Networks.* Englewood Cliffs, NJ: Prentice-Hall.

Tuchman, W.L., and C.H. Meyer. 1978. *Efficacy of the Data Encryption Standard in Data Processing.* New York: IBM Corporation.

U.S. Bureau of Standards. 1986. *Proceedings: National Computer Security Conference 1986.* Washington: GPO, pp. 62–70.

Wood, Charles Cresson. 1986. "Four Roads to Reveal Risk." *Security,* October, pp. 30–32.

Yourdon, Edward. 1986. "Paper Chase Keeping Up With Office Productivity." *Computerworld,* July 21, p. 54.

APPENDIX A

A Management Task List*

This checklist is based on ten years of experience with an international company using sophisticated computing and networking. It is arranged sequentially in the order in which various management processes should be carried out. If your company already has done the steps required in one section, you can skip to the following part.

I.   Information Management
1.   Has a senior manager been assigned responsibility for managing the company's information resource?
     • Senior management recognition of the importance of the information base of the company is a prerequisite to any successful network security effort; the information is the valuable; the network and connected devices are only containers.
2.   Does a company policy define the goals and responsibilities for information management?
     • Policy implies a long-term effort and a consistency of approach; a program in bits and pieces is only a waste of money. The policy should be formally published in an official medium, such as a policy manual or policy guide.
3.   Has the company defined its critical information base and identified the value of information elements therein?
     • Information is a very expensive and critical business resource. One cannot protect everything with any reasonable effectiveness or at acceptable cost; identification of high-value information elements is a requisite to providing practical protection at acceptable cost.
4.   Are company information classification definitions established?
     • The information resource manager must provide a plan for information valuation. The classification scheme provides a way for data owners to conveniently assign information values.
5.   Have information handling regulations been published pertaining to each company information classification?
     • The information handling regulations form the basis for secure practices in the handling of information in all forms.

6. Do information handling regulations specify physical, logical, and procedural protection methods for each information form (written, electronic, mental)?
   - To provide economical and effective protection, management must establish protection requirements for each classification. To protect information while meeting business operating requirements, managers must be able to choose from a menu of security measures.

7. Has information security implementation responsibility been assigned to appropriate managers (for example, administration, information systems, security)?
   - Although all employees are responsible for protecting information, certain managers must be assigned specific responsibilities for program tasks such as classification of basic information elements, construction of protective systems, and implementation of software and hardware controls.

8. Has the company information management executive assigned each of the critical information elements to an information owner?
   - The concept of information ownership is critical to successful implementation of information mangement and protection measures. The information owner must make decisions about information classification and information access and use authorizations. Such authorizations are actually approvals to spend.

9. Have initial information classification decisions been made by the information owners?
   - A first step is necessarily a classification decision about each basic information element. Decisions about element combinations may require consultation among several data owners. These are usually one-time decisions.

10. Do information handling regulations specify a responsibility and process for prompt classification and protection of new company information by its creators (writers of memos, researchers, and so forth)?
    - Innovative or novel information, or new combinations of existing data, may be developed at any time, especially where powerful network-connected workstations are in use. Such information developed during work activities, in the office or at home, may be extremely valuable. Employees must know how to make or obtain prompt classification decisions. Protection is critical during the early stages of the information life cycle.

11. Are controls in place to ensure the erasure or destruction of expired or unneeded electronic business files so as to make the best use of storage resources, and to avoid possible legal exposure during a discovery process?
    - Where LANs are in use, business files may accumulate in file servers. Many files may become obsolete. These files, if not periodi-

cally cleaned out the same as paper files, could be a legal hazard should a lawsuit result in a discovery process.

12. Does the business have contingency plans for continuing operations and recovering lost information in the event of a disaster affecting the information processing infrastructure or data storage facilities?
    - The ability to recover after a serious loss of processing, communications, or data retention capabilities depends on effective detailed planning and practice in plan implementation. The responsibility for recovery is a basic management task.

II. Organization for Security
1. Has the company security manager been assigned responsibility for protection of information in all forms (mental, written, electronic)?
    - The responsibility for protection of business resources should rest with one manager. This is appropriately the company security manager. Information security should not be assigned to the information systems function.
2. Does the company security department have assigned resources to allow the fulfillment of information protection responsibilities (for instance, an information security manager)?
    - The security function must have sufficient expertise to allow the definition of required protection methods for all forms of information. (This does not mean that security software implementation cannot be done by information systems specialists.)
3. Has the security manager established the necessary working relationships with functions associated with information protection efforts (such as information systems technology, general counsel, audit, controller, administration)?
    - The security function must be a part of the ongoing company information management process.

III. Information Security Directives Structure
1. Do company policies define the purpose and ground rules for managing information resources, including information protection?
    - Policy should define all critical requirements but should not include procedural matters.
2. Do information protection policies acknowledge the legal purposes (that is, protection and conservation of proprietary information) of the company's information protection program?
    - Court decisions make it clear that a formal, effective and active information protection program is necessary if a company is to assert its rights to proprietary information (Motorola Inc. v. Fairchild Camera and Instrument Corp., 366 F. Supp. 1173 [D. Ariz. 1973]).
3. Do company information management policies provide for a controlled acceptance of risk?
    - Information protection is not an absolute; business requirements

may dictate that certain risks be taken. Such risk taking should be acknowledged, controlled, and approved by senior management.

4. Is the information policy supported by published information protection standards that cover all aspects of company operations involving information creation, transmittal, communication, processing, storage, and destruction?
    • Information protection standards are the cohesive force in a program for network security. The standards provide the instructions for all employees involved with information resources.

5. Do information protection standards include instructions for identifying, classifying, marking, handling, and protecting information in all forms?
    • Comprehensive standards are important; protection of one form of information and disregard for others is really no protection at all.

6. Are information protection standards published in forms that are appropriate and useful to the various employee groups or classes?
    • Instructions must be made available in forms convenient for use. Secretaries do not need the entire standards package, but their work usually involves much valuable information. A booklet addressed to secretaries might be effective.

7. Do information protection standards address all facets of the company's computing and networking infrastructure?
    • The entire company information processing environment must be covered by standards; the weak link will be the place where the leak occurs.

8. Do information protection standards cover all employee aspects of the use of the company's computer and telecommunications resources?
    • Today we are seeing an information explosion; people are using computer terminals and making telephone calls everywhere, even on airplanes and trains. All these risks must be covered in the standards.

9. Do information standards fix clearly the responsibilities of the various employee classes and groups (managers, supervisors, employees, terminal users, secretaries, personal computer users, and so on)?
    • Each employee must be able to recognize a clear responsibility for taking action to protect company information.

10. Do information protection standards address the company's information interchanges with suppliers, customers, outside counsel, business partners, and foreign countries?
    • Every business passes information to and receives information from outsiders. These exchanges are being automated, and many now take place electronically for reasons of efficiency and economy. There is a severe risk in such activities when company networks become involved.

11. Do information protection standards cover connection with outside networks and data communications services?
    - The use of public data services, airline reservation systems, and value-added carriers may involve some risk to company information resources. Such connections should be evaluated by the security function before a decision on their use is made.
12. Do information protection standards cover the use of company networks by authorized outsiders?
    - For good business reasons, most companies will sooner or later allow outside parties to use the company's networks. Care should be taken to define these outside parties' rights and obligations and to control their activities. A lawsuit after a breach of trust is not really a remedy once information has been exposed.
13. Are information security standards covering the production and distribution of documents followed in company offices and reproduction centers?
14. Do secretaries have current information protection requirement instructions, and are they followed scrupulously?
    - Secretaries are key people in establishing effective information protection practices.
15. Are conflict of interest agreements and disclosure agreements used when appropriate to protect mental information?
    - When company information is provided to employees or contractors, a contract may provide legal remedy should a trust be abused. Agreements define the responsibilities of the parties and, most importantly, help establish the company's rights to its information.
16. Is high value information controlled and tracked throughout its life cycle?
IV. Data Center Security
    1. Do information protection standards specify the protective elements required for company data center facilities and operations?
       - The data center, for most companies, is the information treasure house. It should be protected accordingly.
    2. Are data center facilities strictly controlled, and is access limited to authorized persons?
    3. Are visitors to data centers registered and monitored while on the premises?
    4. Are supervisory responsibilities for security and control spelled out in detail?
       - Rules about security in a dynamic environment can easily be forgotten or ignored. Responsibilities should be clearly defined.
    5. Is media protection and control defined in detail?
       - Tapes and disks should be released from control only under the

most restrictive rules. Used media should not be released unless destroyed if they have been used to store company classified data.

6. Does the data center provide a menu of security services, including data base processor access controls and network information protection measures, for company data processing service users?
   - Systems analysts may recognize information protection needs during application development, but construction of protective measures may be difficult and expensive unless the data center has provided a listing of the standard security offerings available.

7. Is the operations environment tightly controlled (management oversight and approvals for the use of privileged code, update of program libraries, equipment maintenance activities, operating system maintenance activities, and so forth)?
   - An unsupervised computer operations environment is an invitation to fraud.

8. Is dial-up connection to mainframe computers formally controlled through caller identification, authentication, and authorization processes?
   - Dial-up connections are a "worst case" from a security viewpoint. Controls should be in place to positively identify callers and then limit callers to activities specified by data owners.

V. Wide Area Network Security

1. Do information protection standards specify the protective elements required for company wide area network facilities and operations?
   - Wide area networks are often regarded with the same concern as water pipes. This is unfortunate because they constitute a most important resource for the company.

2. Are network operations monitored through an automated control system?

3. Is circuit redundancy provided to ensure continued, reliable operation?

4. Are network facilities secured and physical access limited to authorized persons?
   - All communications facilities, including wiring cabinets, telephone closets, switching rooms, frame rooms, and so forth, in office buildings and other facilities should be carefully secured and all accesses monitored.

5. Are controls in place to identify and authenticate network users?
   - In some cases the network control center may wish to control logical (electronic) access to certain network facilities.

VI. Local Area Network Security

1. Do information protection standards specify the protective elements required for company LAN facilities and operations?
   - Managers may regard LANs as "just another office machine." But

there is a great risk to information, especially when LANs are interconnected. Security elements must be carefully selected to fit the business application and installed before network operation begins.

2. Are LAN installations and applications carefully planned and implemented as a result of diligent systems analysis and business strategies?
   - A LAN should not be installed to see what will happen when it is used. Rather, the installation should be a strategic systems decision based on careful analysis of business requirements, identification of anticipated benefits, and evaluation of the information security vulnerabilities.

3. Do rigorous management actions identify, limit, and control the access privileges of those employees authorized to have access to the network?

4. Are procedures in place to control outsiders (customers, business partners, suppliers, outside counsel) who may have authorized network access?
   - Both questions 3 and 4 above relate to resource management. The incidence of fraudulent or improper use of network facilities by ex-employees (whose authorizations have not been canceled) is astonishing. Access to LANs should not be considered a right, but rather a privilege. Authorized user activities should be monitored, and any change in the employment status or job assignment of an individual (within or outside the company) should result in an immediate suspension of access privileges.

5. Are network support personnel with special privileges limited to reasonable numbers, carefully monitored, and controlled by responsible management?
   - Administrators of LANs have powerful privileges that might easily be used for sabotage or information theft. Careful management attention is required to minimize the number of people with such privileges, to provide suitable security training, and to take action as required in the event of emergency requirements or employee termination or transfer.

6. Are network servers installed in secure areas to prevent unauthorized physical access?
   - Local area network file servers and communications servers are part of the company's information processing infrastructure, just as is the data center, and they deserve equivalent physical protection.

VII. Securing Workstations, Personal Computers, and Terminal Devices

1. Do information protection standards define the management controls over the issuance of network accounts and the provision and use of microcomputers and workstations?

- Network access should be on a need-to-know basis.
2. Do employees have a clear understanding of their responsibilities for protection of company information?
    - With hundreds or thousands of terminal users, the company simply cannot supervise activities; individual employee understanding and motivation are critical.
3. Do employees have appropriate instruction materials (booklets, pamphlets, and so forth) concerning the protection of company information processed or stored in electronic form?
4. Are effective administrative processes in place to ensure the approval, issuance, and cancellation of network and computer use authorities as current employee job responsibilities dictate?
    - The personnel processing activity should result in automatic termination of network authorities whenever an employee changes jobs or is terminated. Some businesses have automated this process by comparing a personnel status file with the network authority file on a daily basis.
5. Are effective procedural and logical processes supporting network/workstation/personal computer user identification and authentication in place?
    - Carefully designed mainframe logical access controls and network clearinghouse controls are essential to fixing individual responsibility for activities. Certain access control software for personal computers or terminals now permits user authentication at the workstation to be interfaced with central computer access control packages. This permits the local user authentication to be used to authorize specified activities on the mainframe computer. Authorization tables (used to allow specific activities to authenticated users) must be maintained so as to be current with business requirements. Administrative processes establish and cancel authorizations in line with employee job assignments.
6. Do information owners formally specify, to the responsible information security function, the individual or group authorities of authenticated information systems users (for instance, to move, read, modify, or delete information)?
    - Data owners are responsible for the use of the information resource entrusted to their care. They meet this responsibility by controlling the use of that resource. This is actually a fiscal responsibility, as every access costs money.
7. Are electronic information devices such as personal computers or workstations provided adequate physical security?
8. Are magnetic media protected and stored as required for the company classification of the information thereon?

- Although many people recognize that papers must be locked away, a surprising loss of information has occurred because the same people failed to lock up disks and tapes.

9. Do employees provide appropriate backup of disks, tapes, and other records essential to business operations?
   - The loss of a master file because of a coffee spill or minor fire could be catastrophic for some business projects or activities centered on local computing.

10. Do users of workstations, personal computers, and other devices properly mark and protect company classified printouts and other documents?
    - Protecting information is always a question when information changes form. Although effective logical controls may be in place to cover the data while in electronic form, a human must make decisions about the data's protection when printed out or displayed.

11. Do personal computer and workstation users follow company rules concerning the use of outside-developed software for processing company classified information?
    - All software has errors, even the best produced by company programmers. Taking a chance on software offered by outsiders is extremely risky; several instances have occurred where such software contained a Trojan horse macro, which eventually destroyed files or caused other damage. A process should be in place to evaluate packages that employees wish to use for business purposes.

12. When downloading data from central database computers, or when uploading results of local processing, do workstation and personal computer users follow applicable company rules?
    - Data integrity is at risk whenever an "official" file is processed locally outside established applications procedures; individual software errors, design errors, definitional differences, and processing carelessness may result in untrustworthy output data. Certainly such data should never be reloaded to the central database.

RECOMMENDED READINGS

For organization and directives structure:
Schweitzer, James A. *Managing Information Security.* Stoneham, MA: Butterworth Publishers, 1982.

For general computing security technology:
Hoffman, Lance J. *Modern Methods for Computer Security and Privacy.* Englewood Cliffs, NJ: Prentice-Hall, 1977.

For information management concepts:
Schweitzer, James A. *Computer Crime and Business Information.* New York: Elsevier Science Publishers, 1986.

For securing workstations:
Schweitzer, James A. *Protecting Information in the Electronic Workplace.* Englewood Cliffs, NJ: Prentice-Hall, 1984.

APPENDIX B

An Automated Logical Access Control Standard*

Charles R. Symons and James A. Schweitzer

For most business** data processed or communicated via computers, ensuring satisfactory security requires awkward compromises. Most business data are not sufficiently valuable that they need the sort of security measures that banks and the military typically employ to protect critical or private data. The intrinsic value of much financial or government information may make it worthwhile for a criminal to invest a large amount of money to steal a much larger sum, or obtain state secrets. Security measures, therefore, tend to be complex and thus expensive. For example, encryption is widely used to protect data in storage and transmission.

Most routine business data however, do not warrant elaborate, expensive security protection. Indeed, security may be given a much lower priority than the goal of making the company's data easily accessible to large populations of users who need it for their jobs. As the costs of on-line working and office automation fall steadily compared with other costs, more and more employees are given direct access from personal workstations in their office, or from home or other remote, physically insecure locations via dial-up or direct connection to their data on business computers.

This same drive to improve accessibility, however, can also improve the chances of successful penetration of the computer system by unauthorized users. Basic business control reasons mean that some need-to-know restrictions on access are inevitably needed even for authorized employees. Also, some categories of business data, such as personal data or commercially sensitive financial forecasts on product specifications, may require special security.

But business computers must also be secure against the attention of people whose hobby is to try and break in and browse around or trespass within computers. Recent frequent reports in the media indicate that this is a growing threat that must be taken seriously. Public concern has reached the point that the computer industry must respond to this threat.

**We use the term *business* in the widest sense, covering both for profit and nonprofit organizations.

Summarizing the conflicting pressures on computer security, a typical business data processing or automated office community requires its computers and workstations to have a security system that:

- Is reasonably priced consistent with business information values; everyone wants the payroll kept secret, but no one wants to spend much to protect it.
- Offers minimal bureaucracy to the user community that wants only to get at their data.
- Requires only minimal effort on the part of managers of the data processing service who do not want to have an expensive security administration or policing function; this suggests using the power of the computer itself to do the job.
- Is reasonably effective against the threats of carelessness, inquisitiveness, computer trespassing via networks, temptation to commit fraud, and so on.

The security/cost/nuisance compromise that must be reached, therefore, lies somewhere between the "Fort Knox" and "Open House" extremes. A security barrier that is obviously going to require a significant effort to penetrate will deter most computer trespassers. It does not have to be a perfect barrier.

Computer security measures are normally considered under the headings physical security, procedural security, and logical access security. The first two headings are well understood but are becoming relatively less important. When computers can be accessed from large numbers of remote terminals, users will be able to obtain business information without being physically present on the business premises or subject to procedural controls. Logical access security measures are those hardware and software processes that control access to data within computing systems for business control, privacy, and security purposes.

The purpose of this appendix, therefore, is to examine the logical access security measures that a user, whether authorized or not, of a business data processing computer should encounter before he or she can start useful work. An optimum set of logical access controls is proposed, and for reasons that will become apparent, a standard set of controls, automatically enforced by the computer, is recommended. The standard has been named Automated Logical Access Control Standard, or ALACS.

LOGICAL ACCESS CONTROL EFFECTIVENESS

Standard commercial logical access control software designed to protect business data normally puts three steps in the way of the user who wants to sign on to the computer and perform certain tasks. These are:

1. **Identification.** The user is required to enter a valid and uniquely identifying code, or UserID. This could be, for example, a personnel number; it commonly doubles as an account code.

2. **Authentication.** Having been identified, the user is required to provide some code or token that is privately known or personally held, to authenticate that the user is really who he or she claims to be. This could be a plastic card, fingerprint, or recognizable voice pattern. By far the most common authentication means is for the user to enter a private password. From here on we shall consider only passwords as authentication means. Other forms of token may become common in the future, but that will not change the validity of our position on passwords.

3. **Authorization.** The authenticated user is then permitted to perform only those actions—for example, access and update certain files, execute certain programs or transactions, read certain documents—that have been preauthorized.

To examine the security effectiveness of logical access control mechanisms in preventing unauthorized access, we must again consider these three logical steps independently.

First, the UserID has a limited security role. If a personnel code such as an employee number is chosen to be used for the UserID, then such codes may be general knowledge within the organization. UserIDs are often required to be entered in cleartext and can therefore be seen by passersby or obtained from printout. If doubling as an account code, they will appear on invoices for computer usage that may pass through many hands. UserIDs that become known to employees who leave the business, as well as to contract staff, visitors, and so on, effectively become public knowledge. Thus, although it serves to distinguish each individual who may use the computer, a UserID may have no security value at all; it represents (only) a "claim to be" a certain person.

The authenticating password is a different matter. If the password is properly constructed, and if the user keeps it secret and private, not easily guessable, and changes it periodically, then a password can provide a highly effective security mechanism. The crucial word, of course, is *if*. It is a matter of common knowledge within large data processing installations, confirmed by published articles in computer journals (see, for example, R. Morris and K. Thompson, "Password Security: A Case History," *Communications of ACM,* November 1979) and by newspaper stories of computer break-ins (see, for example, "Trial and Error by Intruders Led to Entry Into Computers," *New York Times,* 23 August 1983), that user password discipline is often poor. Passwords are written down, easily guessable strings or names associated with the user. Passwords are seldom changed, and then only as a result of enforcement exercises by the security or data processing management.

The third logical element, authorization processes, is usually well designed and enforceable. Time-sharing systems, for example, will commonly allow an authenticated user to access only public program libraries or data and programs that he or she has personally entered or created. Extension of access rights to other users requires some positive action on the part of the data owner or a security administrator. Likewise, properly designed transaction-processing systems can be made completely inaccessible to a given UserID unless that UserID has been specifically authorized to execute certain transactions by a security administrator. Authorization mechanisms have received the greatest attention by designers of security systems. For example, the U.S. Department of Defense's "Trusted Computer System Evaluation Criteria" concentrates very heavily on authorization mechanisms.[1] Generally speaking, therefore, at reasonably low administrative overhead cost, authorization rights to access data can be automatically enforced and do not interfere unduly with business data processing needs.

It is obvious from the foregoing that the weak link in the chain of logical access security is the password. Users of business data processing services are motivated much more by their desire to get on with their computing than by a concern for data security (generally users have a low perception of risk consistent with management views); password discipline is not normally enforced, and hence password discipline is poor.

Attempting to enforce password discipline by exhortation or supervisory methods is ineffective. In today's business conditions the policing of a large population of users with terminals at home and elsewhere is not practicable. Such an effort is in any case unpopular, as it smacks of bureaucracy.

This analysis and line of reasoning led to the idea of developing a specification that would require the computer itself to enforce logical access security, automatically, as fast as possible, at each stage of use from sign-on to sign-off. The specification should pay particular attention to enforcing password discipline.

AUTOMATED LOGICAL ACCESS CONTROL STANDARD

ALACS has as its objective to specify an optimum set of logical access controls in order to provide adequate security for typical confidential business data; these controls are to be automatically enforced by the computer's operating system and, if necessary, supplemented by the application system. Where not automatically enforceable because of system limitations, ALACS should provide maximum computer assistance for the manual administration of security.

A full specification of ALACS is given at the end of this Appendix, and the security objective for each requirement is explained.

It should be emphasized that ALACS contains no new security features that have not at some time been proposed or implemented by some computer supplier. Many of the requirements for passwords are described in a FIPS publication.[2]

---

[1]U.S. Department of Defense, "Trusted Computer System Evaluation Criteria," U.S. Department of Defense Computer Security Center, 24 May 1982.

[2]"Guideline on User Authentication Techniques for Computer Network Access Control," FIPS (Federal Information Processing Standards) Publication, PUB 83, 29 September 1980.

However, a survey of the logical access controls of twelve software systems from seven unique combinations of leading hardware/software suppliers showed that none met ALACS completely, and most had several significant weaknesses.

The novelty of ALACS is only that it covers all aspects of logical access control requirements for typical business data in one statement and that it specifies a sign-on protocol that maximizes automatic enforcement of password discipline in a user-friendly way. The parts of ALACS concerned with access authorization mechanisms are already standard practice on many suppliers' computer systems.

Publishing ALACS as a proposed standard serves two goals: First, in the short term, an organization can compare its existing computer logical access control mechanisms with ALACS as a means of identifying weaknesses in security effectiveness. These weaknesses can then be rectified by in-house software modifications and/or brought to the computer supplier's attention; alternatively the risk of the weakness can be consciously accepted. At best, security is improved; at worst, awareness of security vulnerability is heightened.

Second, in the longer-term, ALACS should stimulate debate in the business data processing community, and especially standardization bodies. The debate will no doubt produce suggestions for improvements to ALACS. With increased customer pressure and public concern arising from the computer trespassing threat, computer manufacturers and suppliers of security packages should find it worthwhile to implement ALACS fully.

A full and uniform implementation of ALACS would not only bring a great improvement in computer security over the current level, it would generally help make computers easier to use. Today each business computer system has its own unique sign-on procedure and security mechanism. Imagine the parallel if every time you rented a car it was necessary to get out a manual to work out how to start the engine and drive off. Car manufacturers have evolved a standard user-friendly man–machine interface, and increasingly that interface incorporates safety-enforcement mechanisms (such as reminders about seat-belt wearing), analogous to ALACS' requiring computers to enforce security. Although *standard* in a conceptual sense, each car's interface is realized in practice in a unique way as far as detailed presentation and aesthetics are concerned. Likewise, ALACS is a conceptual specification. Details of presentation are left to the implementor.

A standard such as ALACS, therefore, has wider implications than security. The improvements in computer-user acceptability and productivity, which would follow wide-scale implementation of ALACS, especially for large organizations using computers from many suppliers, will in the long term be as valuable as its security benefit.

Objective

To specify an optimum set of logical processes that can be implemented on a computer to control access to confidential data and text held on the computer for the purposes of maintaining adequate security.

Scope

1. Any computer whose use is shared by a closed community of users, any of whom may use the computer and/or access files via terminals, microcomputers, and so on, for certain preauthorized purposes,
2. Where the data or text that are held are either
    a. confidential to the organization or part of the organization using the computer and/or
    b. subject to other need-to-know restrictions—for example, for internal control reasons, personal privacy, and so on.

Terminology

In this standard the word *computer* is used to encompass any computer, system or subsystem, shared intelligent workstation, or group or network thereof, with which a user communicates, in interactive or batch mode, and which is a separate entity from a security control viewpoint. The controls described within ALACS may be distributed over various processors within the computer, as appropriate to its configuration and security needs.

Requirements

The following minimum requirements must be met. For each requirement the corresponding security objective is given alongside.

Requirement	Security Objective
A. **UserID.** A UserID, minimum six characters, must be assigned to each individual user, which is unique to that computer. The computer will not allow two or more terminals to be signed on simultaneously with the same UserID.	Inhibits sharing of UserIDs and emphasizes individual accountability for usage and security.
Although assigned to an individual person, a UserID may belong to one or more recognized groups of UserIDs that share common access authorizations. (See C.2.a below.)	Helps simplify administration of access authorizations.
B. **Passwords.** Each individual UserID must have an associated password, which the user is instructed to keep private with the following characteristics:	Password is the key to authenticating that the user is indeed the individual identified by the UserID.

Requirement	*Security Objective*
1. **Length.** Minimum of 6 alphanumeric or special characters, excluding blanks.	Makes password harder to guess by trial and error or to discover from systematic testing.
2. **Frequency of change.** The computer will force a password to be changed within D days of the last change, where D is an installation parameter with maximum ninety-nine days, default thirty days.	Forced password changing reduces the security exposure if an existing password has become known to persons other than the password owner. Forced changing also heightens general user security consciousness.
3. **Repeatability.** The computer will maintain a list of the last P passwords used by the UserID and will not accept an attempt to change to a password already used and still in the list. P is an installation parameter with a minimum of ten passwords.	Inhibits the user's trying to beat the enforced password changing control.
4. **Initialization.** When a new UserID is established, it will be given an "expired" password (see C.1.c below)—that is, one that must be changed at the first attempted sign-on by the UserID.	Prevents the person allocating UserIDs from knowing the password that will be used by the user concerned.
5. **Encryption.** All passwords will be stored in the computer in one-way encrypted form. A password entered during an interactive sign-on or a batch job submission will be immediately encrypted at the time of entry, and thereafter never displayed in cleartext.	Prevents a system programmer or someone working in "privileged" mode (see C.3 below) from obtaining passwords and thereby being able to impersonate any UserID.
C. **Logical Access Control**	
1. **Sign-on (Identification/Authentication) Phase** Sign-on will follow the procedure below, from the point where the computer is ready to accept identification of the user via a UserID.	
a. Computer invites sign-on by requesting entry of the UserID in an indicated field. If accepted, the computer proceeds with step b. If not accepted, the computer allows up to two more attempted entries, and then if still unsuccessful:	Procedure is designed to help the genuine user but inhibit someone trying to find an acceptable UserID by trial and error.

(continued)

Requirement	*Security Objective*

• logs all unsuccessfully tried UserIDs;
    • alerts operator or system security administrator;
    • (if appropriate) disconnects the terminal.	

b. Computer invites entry of password, in an indicated field, but provides a "blot" (or inhibits display or printing) for that field so that the entered password cannot be read. User enters password, and if successful, the computer proceeds with step c. If unsuccessful, the computer allows up to two more attempted entries, and if still unsuccessful:
    • logs all unsuccessfully tried passwords;
    • alerts operator or system security administrator;
    • (if appropriate) disconnects the terminal.
	Procedure is designed to help the genuine user but inhibit a casual observer from seeing the password or someone trying to guess a password by trial and error.

N.B. The computer should enforce a time delay of at least two seconds between repeated attempted entries of a password.	Inhibits someone successfully using a computer to generate passwords systematically to gain entry.
c. The computer checks if today the password is more than E days from the date of expiration (E is an installation parameter, usually set to 20 percent of the forced change period D). If the password is still more than E days from the expiration, the computer proceeds with step f.	To be as helpful as possible the computer gives advance warning to a user whose password is due to expire imminently.
d. If the password is within E days of expiration but is still unexpired, the computer issues a warning giving the number of days remaining before the password must be changed. Alternatively, if the password expires today or is already expired, the computer informs the user that the password must be changed immediately.	

Requirement	*Security Objective*
e. The computer issues an invitation to change the password, indicating the format and supplying a "blot" (or inhibiting display or printing). The user may ignore the invitation to change by pressing Return unless the password is already expired or expires today. If the user enters a new password, the computer invites a repeat entry to validate the first entry (similarly concealed) and continues until two successive identical passwords are entered.	The computer helps the user change password and enforces change of an expired password. A changed password is requested a second time to avoid problems that would be caused by a typing error during the first entry and to reinforce the new password in the user's memory.
f. The computer issues a message stating the date and time when the last successful sign-on was made.	Provides a check for the user that his or her UserID has not been used without the user's knowledge.
Batch Job or message submission from an interactive terminal or workstation:	
g. The computer will allow a batch job or message to be submitted for execution or sent from an interactive terminal or workstation only if the batch job or message is associated with the same UserID/password combination used for initial sign-on.	Prevents a user from signing on under one UserID with associated authorizations and then creating and submitting a job with a different authorization.
h. Sign-on proceeds essentially as in interactive mode, except the computer does not provide guiding messages and if any step is unsuccessful, the job is canceled, with the appropriate explanation	
2. Processing (Authorization) Phase	
a. Any computer to which the UserID may gain access will control, using information provided by the owner of the object concerned:	Each UserID should be limited in what use can be made of the computer by pre-agreed need-to-know considerations.
• The list of objects (programs, transactions, files,	

(continued)

Requirement	*Security Objective*

etc.) to which the UserID is allowed access either individually or by virtue of membership of a recognized group or of preregistered attributes.

- The level of access (read, copy, update, create/delete, execute) allowed to the objects.

Additionally, the computer will warn the user (interactive mode) or cancel the job (batch mode) if the user tries to access beyond the authorized range or levels.

b. The list of UserIDs, or recognized groups of UserIDs, that may access any object and the associated level of access may be changed only by
- the UserID that individually created the object,
- the object's owner (if such is established), or
- the system security administrator working in privileged access mode (see below).

The rules and mechanisms for changing access authorizations must be clearly and coherently established; they will vary depending on the type of computing service. Time-sharing and office systems usually allow only the creator of an object to change the access authorizations. In contrast, a community of users sharing a common data base is better regulated via a system security administrator acting on behalf of the data base owner.

c. Any major subsystem executing on the computer that is shared by users with different need-to-know requirements and is treated as a single object by the computer's security system must itself provide its own authorization scheme along the lines of 2.a above.

The computer's security system may not be able to cope with incompatible security conventions of a "foreign" subsystem. The latter must therefore provide its own authorization mechanisms.

d. If a terminal or workstation is inactive for more than T minutes, the associated UserID will be automatically signed off. T will be an installation parameter with a default of fifteen minutes.

Prevents someone from using a terminal that has been left by a user who forgot to sign off.

As an alternative to sign-off, the computer blanks the terminal screen and requires reen-

Alternative caters to the case where the overhead due to sign-on/sign-off is unacceptable.

Requirement	Security Objective

try of the user's password to resume the session.

3. Privileged Access

A privileged access mode will be available to a system security administrator for maintenance of all security and logical access control parameters, but only for those purposes. Privileged access will not be needed for any application programming or use of an application or utility program.

A privileged access mode is essential for security administration, such as establishing and deleting UserIDs, changing certain types of access authorizations, etc. Such a privileged access mode must itself be protected from unauthorized use to at least the ALACS standard.

4. Logging

All unsuccessful sign-on attempts and all unsuccessful access attempts during processing (both of range and levels) will be recorded in a log in the computer concerned, available only in privileged access mode. All log message types will be uniquely coded, and date and time stamped to enable analysis. Analysis programs will highlight suspicious repeatedly unsuccessful sign-on or acccess attempts.

A log of attempted security violations is an essential defense mechanism to help a system security administrator discover apparent deliberate attempted violations.

5. Authorization Maintenance

Administrative procedures will be established for each computer such that:

a. If an individual leaves the organization, any individual UserID is immediately canceled.

b. If an individual's job is changed, then any consequential changes of the individual's authorization to access programs, transactions, data, etc., are immediately affected.

Sound procedures to administer UserIDs are an essential counterpart to the computer-enforceable security measures.

D. Optional Refinements

1. Physical Terminal constrained to certain UserIDs. The computer may allow only certain UserIDs to sign on to certain physical terminals.

This is a valuable option for situations where specific computer processing should be possible only from certain terminals that could be at a specific secure location, equipped with certain security features, etc., due to the need to handle particularly sensitive data.

(continued)

Requirement	Security Objective
2. Dial-up. An indication of whether or not access via a dial-up port is allowed will be associated with each UserID. An attempt to use dial-up when not authorized will result in failure to sign on.	Anyone wanting to obtain a UserID/password combination by trial and error will probably need the privacy of a remote dial-up link to make the attempt. Therefore, limiting dial-up access to known users who have valid reasons for dial-up can limit this security risk.
3. Unused UserIDs. If a UserID is unused for more than say ninety days, the computer logs that fact so that the system security administrator can ascertain whether the UserID is still needed.	A valuable aid for the system security administrator in isolating potentially defunct UserIDs.

APPENDIX C

A Problem Reporting
and Resolution Procedure

SCOPE

All problems associated with services that occur or are identified at any site (local, area, or zone level) worldwide.

OBJECTIVE

To provide a procedure that will facilitate the identification, investigation, and solution of all problems relating to services.

RESPONSIBILITIES

General

The prime responsibility for problem reporting rests with users; all problems experienced by users and not resolved by them mut be reported (by whatever means is defined locally) to the assigned local support center (LSC). The responsibilities of local, area, and zone support centers are defined in the corporate standard entitled *Internet Management*.

Specific

Problem Reporting

All service problems must be reported formally to the LSC only when the user is satisfied that correct operating procedures, as defined in the appropriate product/service documentation, have been followed. Where possible, problem reporting must include sufficient information to permit the reproduction of the problem by the LSC. Note: For service problems first identified at area or zone level, that level will assume responsibility for all activities normally performed at lower levels.

Logging and Status Reporting

LSCs are responsible for maintaining records of all reported service problems and for advising the user concerned of all progress, final resolution, and/or workarounds.

Investigating

Area support centers (ASCs) must communicate with one another (within and between zones), with area local OIS and telecommunications support personnel, with Xerox and other vendor support staffs, and with zone support center (ZSC) personnel in order to formulate, agree on, and implement diagnostic action plans; they must pursue each problem until it is resolved and keep the reporting LSC informed of progress at all times.

Solving

Responsibility for solving all problems, or identifying workaround actions and taking escalating action, rests with ASCs.

Escalating

If an ASC is unable to solve a problem, having invoked all the assistance available to it, it must document the problem, its symptoms, and the results of the investigative actions and submit a full report to the appropriate ZSC. If the ZSC is unable to obtain a solution to the problem, it will pass this report to the Product Support Consulting Office (PSCO) and communicate with this unit until a solution is identified or provided.

Documentation

ASCs are responsible for preparing and issuing procedures defining the way in which:

- Users report problems to LSCs.
- LSCs maintain records of reported problems.
- LSCs report problems to their ASC.

ZSCs are responsible for preparing and issuing a procedure defining the way in which problems will be escalated to them by their ASCs.

The PSCO is responsible for preparing and issuing a procedure defining the way in which ZSCs will escalate problems to it.

PROCEDURE

Each ZSC is responsible for developing a detailed problem resolution and reporting procedure that will incorporate the following.

Problem Investigation

- Reproduction of the problem.
- Use of available diagnostic tools.
- Identification of local or remote hardware and software faults.
- Identification of wide area network (WAN) telecommunications faults.
- Redirection of service problems to the appropriate support organization.

Diagnostic Support

- Role of telecoms support.
- Role of local OIS support.
- Role of outside vendors.
- Role of other ASCs.
- Role of ZSC.
  - Identification of ASC contacts.
  - Provision of technical advice.
  - Responsibility for WAN trunk facilities.
  - Responsibility for zone facilities.
  - Help desk services.

Problem Logging

- Each ZSC will enter all known problems into a problem data base.
- This data base, which can be accessed remotely by any LSC or ASC, will be held in the zone library.
- The ZSC is responsible for making regular exchanges of reports between zones and for ensuring that they obtain copies of product problem resolution reports.

GLOSSARY

AR Action request. The formal report of problems (hardware and software).
Area A subdivision of a zone. Within the management hierarchy the area support center (ASC) is the principal focus for user problem solving and is accountable to the user community served by that area for the availability and quality of the services provided.
OIS Office Information Systems.
Zone A geographical area that for purposes of operational management and service enhancement planning is treated as a separate entity.

Index